Ethics and Genetics

Teaching Ethics: Material for Practitioner Education (TEMPE)

General Editor: Donna Dickenson, John Ferguson Professor at the University of Birmingham and Director of the Centre for the Study of Global Ethics

These three books introduce key areas in current medical ethics to readers with no previous knowledge in the field. Structured around a variety of guided activities and real-life cases, the books look respectively at the implications of the possible abuses of new reproductive technologies, "new genetics", and protection of research subjects in an increasingly global environment of research trials. Both authors and cases represent a wide range of European backgrounds and professional disciplines, including medicine, bioethics, law, sociology, theology, and philosophy. A video further enhances the value of these workbooks.

Volume 1

Ethics of New Reproductive Technologies: Cases and Questions

Dolores Dooley, Joan McCarthy, Tina Garanis-Papadatos, Panagiota Dalla-Vorgia +

Volume 2

Ethics and Genetics: A Workbook for Practitioners and Students

Guido de Wert, Ruud ter Meulen, Roberto Mordacci, Mariachiara Tallacchini

Volume 3

Issues in Medical Research Ethics

Jürgen Boomgaarden, Pekka Louhiala, Urban Wiesing

Ethics and Genetics

A Workbook for Practitioners and Students

Guido de Wert
Ruud ter Meulen
Roberto Mordacci
Mariachiara Tallacchini

Berghahn Books
New York • Oxford

First published in 2003 by **Berghahn Books**
www.BerghahnBooks.com

©2003 Guido de Wert
Ruud ter Meulen
Roberto Mordacci
Mariachiara Tallacchini

Library of Congress Cataloging-in-Publication Data

Ethics and genetics : a workbook for practitioners and students /
Guido de Wert ... [et al.].
    p. cm. -- (Teaching Ethics: Material for Practitioner Education; vol. 2)
    Includes bibliographical references and index.
    ISBN 1-57181-600-3 (hardback : alk. paper)
    1. Medical genetics--Moral and ethical aspects. 2. Human genetics--
Research--Moral and ethical aspects. I. Wert, Guido de. II. Teaching
ethics (New York) ; vol. 2.

RB155 .E797 2003
174' .29042--dc21

British Library Cataloguing in Publication Data

A catalogue record for this book is available from the British Library
Printed in the United States on acid-free paper

ISBN 1-57181-600-3 hardback

Contents

Foreword

TEMPE is a two-year research project (2000–2002) funded by the European Commission Framework-5 Programme. TEMPE is an umbrella title for research, workshops, text composition and video production on three themes: Ethics in New Reproductive Technologies, Genetics and Medical Research. The lead coordinator of TEMPE is Professor Donna Dickenson, formerly at Imperial College School of Medicine, London. Professor Dickenson's experience with a previous open-learning BIOMED-2 project proved invaluable in advising the process of developing TEMPE. Associate partner-researchers for the three themes come from a variety of disciplines at third level institutions in Greece, Ireland, Germany, Finland, Italy, the Netherlands and the United Kingdom. The project focuses on the development of a set of distance-learning workbooks on these three core themes in health care ethics, for use on a Europe-wide basis. A unique feature of TEMPE is that it devolves the production of the case-based textbooks for health care ethics to associate partners.

The following text, 'Ethics of Genetics', is the result of a partnership between Imperial College, London; the Universita San Raffaele, Milan; and the Institute for Bioethics, Maastricht. Guido de Wert of the Institute for Bioethics was responsible for Chapter 1 and 2; Mariachiara Tallachini and Roberto Mordacci of San Raffaele were responsible for Chapter 3; Ruud ter Meulen was responsible for Chapter 4 and Roberto Mordacci, Mariachiara Tallachini and Ruud ter Meulen were responsible for Chapter 5. Ruud ter Meulen was responsible for the coordination of the project 'Ethics of Genetics', while Donna Dickenson was responsible for the supervision of the project.

The authors of this text acknowledge the contribution of all participants in the two workshops on 'Ethics and Genetics' held in Maastricht (June 2000) and Milan (November

2000), as well as the contribution of the participants in the users' workshop in Maastricht (September 2001). Those who have contributed specific cases, commentaries on cases or pieces of text are acknowledged in the text itself and in the references. A complete list of all participants in the three workshops appears at the end of this workbook.

The authors acknowledge the comments of the critical readers to the first draft of the workbook. A full list of the critical readers appears at the end of this workbook.

Maastricht – Milan, 17 December 2001.

Introduction

Genetic information plays an increasingly important role in our lives. As a result of the Human Genome Project, our knowledge of the genetic basis of various diseases is increasing, with important consequences for the role of genetics in clinical practice, health care systems and for society at large.

In a clinical setting, genetic testing may result in better insight into susceptibility to inheritable diseases, not only before or after birth, but also at later stages in life. In addition to prenatal testing and preconception testing, predictive testing has also progressively increased and has resulted in new possibilities for the early treatment and prevention of inheritable diseases. However, not all inheritable diseases which can be predicted on the basis of genetic information can be treated or cured. Should we offer genetic tests to persons for untreatable diseases? In general, we say no, but what to do with people who want to know their genetic status? Should we inform family members about the results of genetic tests of individuals, even when there are no options for treatment? What, in such cases, is the role of the 'right not to know'? Should we inform family members when there is only an increased risk of contracting a disease?

We have mentioned a few examples of ethical questions in the area of predictive and prenatal testing. While these types of testing are oriented towards the individual (and his or her family), genetic screening is practised at the level of populations. The objective of genetic screening is to detect the genetic conditions of diseases for which no history or other indications are present. Genetic screening can take place before conception, birth, just after birth, or later in life. One of the ethical problems with screening is whether family members and relatives should be informed. What actually is the role of the informed consent of the target population? Another issue is the selection of screening programmes for genetic dispositions: for which diseases do we set up screening programmes?

The ethical problems with clinical genetics are to a large extent to do with the probabilistic character of genetic information. Though for *some* diseases (like Huntington's disease), one can predict with certainty the onset of the disease, for many others one can not. Tests for heart disease or cancer, for example, are not very accurate, as these diseases are often influenced by environmental factors and the lifestyle or health behaviour of the person tested. The unpredictability and complexity of multifactorial genetic diseases, as well as the controversies about the reliability of some existing tests, make genetic information very challenging material for both the individual and society. Decisions on the basis of genetic information are always based on an assessment of possible risks and benefits. Genetic decisions, in individual and social cases, are decisions under conditions of uncertainty.

One could argue that, as the predictive value of genetic knowledge is generally low or moderate, it is not specifically different from other kinds of medical information. However, there is one big difference between genetic and other medical information, which is the fact that genetic information is not confined to an individual. Because of their genetic make-up, individuals are linked with each other, not only within families but also in larger communities and populations. This means that genetic data cannot be merely considered as, and reduced to, a matter of individual choice; in decisions on genetic testing, screening and research, one must always be aware of both the interests of the individual and of the interests of other persons who are genetically linked to him or her.

The social character of genetic information and decision making on the basis of this information is reflected in the structure of this workbook. The book starts with a chapter on reproductive genetic counselling, prenatal testing and preimplantation testing. Though decisions in this area are very much based on the autonomy of prospective parents, possible links with family networks can become relevant here. Chapter 2 proceeds with the ethics of predictive genetic testing, i.e., testing for disorders that manifest themselves later in life. Family networks become more relevant here, as decisions by individuals to be tested for late onset diseases will in some way or another affect the interests and wellbeing of family members. Chapter 3 deals with genetic population screening and genetic community research. The perspective of a community makes explicit the fact that genetic information does not only involve the individuals undergoing screening, but is also relevant to families and communities as a whole. Chapter 4 presents the ethical issues regarding the social use of genetic information, particularly the use of genetic information for access to (private) insurance and the workplace. Genetic testing may give insurance companies a powerful tool to get insight not only into the genetic heritage of the individual applicant but into the genetic heritage of his or her family as well. Future applications of family members and other relatives may be seriously impeded by the information that insurers have stored about one individual applicant. The workbook ends with a chapter containing theoretical reflections on uncertainty in genetic clinical practice, as well as the social character of genetic information. As can be noted in the workbook, the principle of respect for autonomy, which is an important ethical principle in clinical genetics, may interfere with respect for the interests and autonomy of other persons, like family members. Do we then need a new paradigm for the ethics of genetics? How should we interpret the probabilistic nature of genetic information? Are we our genes? Or are we, because of the nature of genetic information, *not* our genes?

– 1 –

Ethics of Reproductive Genetic Counselling, Prenatal and Preimplantation Testing

Clinical genetics have traditionally concentrated on reproductive genetic counselling. For this reason, this workbook opens with a chapter on ethical issues related to this type of counselling. The first section addresses the implications of the ideal of nondirectiveness. The second section focuses on ethical aspects of prenatal diagnosis, in particular on the implications of the right not to know and the right to know. The ethics of preimplantation genetic diagnosis are discussed in the third and final section.

Objectives

After reading this chapter you will be able to:

- understand the relevant moral issues of reproductive genetic counselling.
- clarify the professional responsibilities of the genetic counsellor with respect to advising on reproductive choices.
- weigh the arguments 'pro' and 'con' the ideal of nondirectiveness in genetic reproductive counselling.

- analyse the ethical issues of prenatal diagnosis from the viewpoints of consequentialist and deontological theories.
- assess the moral weight of the 'right to know' and the 'right not to know' of (prospective) parents regarding the genetic condition of their (unborn) child.
- evaluate from a moral point of view the criteria for parental access to prenatal diagnosis, including willingness or unwillingness to consider an abortion.
- evaluate from a moral viewpoint the indications for preimplantation genetic diagnosis.

Reproductive Autonomy and the Ideal of Non-directive Counselling

The case of Tim and Marian

Tim is a carrier of Huntington's disease. He and his wife Marian are hesitating over whether they want to have children. On the one hand, there is a high risk (50 percent) of inheritance for the child. But on the other hand, the chance that the child will not inherit the mutation is equally high. Furthermore, while Huntington's disease is currently untreatable, in the future therapeutic interventions might be available. For the moment, they are not sure which option they prefer: take the risk; refrain from having children; adopt a child; artificial insemination with donor sperm; or prenatal diagnosis.

Huntington's disease is a neurodegenerative disorder. The pattern of inheritance is autosomal dominant, which means that children of a patient have a 50 percent risk of inheriting the mutation. All carriers of the mutation will get the disease – the 'penetrance' of the mutation is complete. Huntington's disease has a midlife onset and is untreatable. Patients usually die approximately 15–20 years after the onset of the disorder.

Activity:

Clearly, Tim and Marian have to face difficult questions. Basically, the choice is between just taking the risk or taking 'preventive' measures. Tim and Marian are wrestling with the moral implications of this choice – 'What is responsible parenthood?' Do you think that Tim and Marian are morally obliged to take preventive measures? Make a list of arguments for and against.

In modern Western culture, there is a (strong) consensus that the reproductive freedom of prospective parents should be respected and protected – that the state should not interfere in reproductive matters. This so-called 'right of liberty' also applies to prospective parents at high risk of conceiving an affected child.

At the same time, there is an ongoing ethical debate about the meaning and implications of 'responsible parenthood': should prospective high risk parents, from a moral *(not legal)* point of view, take steps to avoid having an affected child? There is little support for the view that prospective parents should take into account primarily societal, particularly economic, interests – a view that would entail an economic rationalisation of the notion 'responsible parenthood'. The ethical debate concentrates on the question of whether prospective parents at high risk of having a child with (or carrying) a serious disorder should avoid harm/suffering to the future child (Brock 1995).

Assessing the ethical dimensions of reproductive choices is a complex, difficult and controversial task (Arras 1990). We must first identify the crucial elements of any assessment and then attempt to weigh and balance them against one another. Important elements include:

a) the magnitude of the threatened harm,
b) the probability of the harm actually occurring, and
c) the ability and willingness of parents to assume their proper responsibility for the future child.

The task of weighing is complicated by the absence of clearly defined standards within each rubric (e.g., 'What risks for progeny are acceptable?') and by the absence of a well-established rule for ranking the importance of each element. In view of this, it is no surprise that reasonable people will often evaluate concrete reproductive choices in a different way.

Activity:

Would you now, in view of the three morally relevant variables just mentioned, come to another conclusion regarding the moral dilemma faced by Tim and Marian?

What about the responsibility or task of doctors/professionals involved in the genetic counselling of clients at risk of transmitting a particular disorder? Your answer probably depends, at least in part, upon your view about the nature and goal(s) of reproductive genetic counselling.

Activity:

What do you think is the primary goal of reproductive genetic counselling? Confront your view with the position of the American Society of Human Genetics presented below.

The American Society of Human Genetics (1975) defined genetic counselling as a communication process which deals with the human problems associated with the occurrence, or risk of occurrence, of a genetic disorder in a family. This process involves an attempt by one or more appropriately trained persons to help the individual or family:

1) comprehend the facts, including the diagnosis, the probable course of the disorder and the available methods of management.
2) appreciate the way heredity contributes to the disorder, and the risk of recurrence in specified relatives.
3) understand the options for dealing with the risk of recurrence.
4) choose the course of action which seems appropriate to them in view of their risk and their family goals and act in accordance with that decision.
5) make the best possible adjustment to the disorder in an affected member and/or to the risk of recurrence of that disorder.

The professional standards of clinical geneticists/genetic counsellors stress the importance of so-called *non-directiveness* to promote the client's reproductive autonomy (Andrews et al. 1994, British Medical Association 1998). The counsellor has a professional duty to create an atmosphere where clients can make choices based on their own beliefs, values and preferences. Furthermore, counsellors should provide unconditional support, whatever the clients decide. Clients at high risk of having an affected child should be able to decide whether to have or not to have genetic testing, and they should be able to decide how to use the information and/or test results they receive as they see best. Their options include: to take the risk, to adopt a child, the use of donor gametes, prenatal diagnosis and, sometimes, preimplantation genetic diagnosis. The counsellor should not give his personal view, at least not unsolicited.

To give unsolicited advice, to give one's personal opinion, is, according to the Ethics Committee of the Royal Dutch Society of Physicians, unwarranted and unwise, for various reasons (1997):

1. Recommending any particular course of action undermines the autonomy of the individual client (even though unsolicited advice is not necessarily a usurpation of the client's decision making authority).
2. There is no gold standard for 'genetic responsibility' or 'responsible parenthood'. Reasonable people may regularly disagree about acceptable 'harm-probability' ratios.
3. Directive counselling entails a revival of the classical role of the eugenically motivated 'gatekeeper' – which might increase the resistance to genetic counselling.

Activity:

Can you think of any counterarguments that might be used against this position?

While there is a strong consensus that non-directiveness is an important value/ideal, there is an ongoing debate concerning its precise meaning and implications. Here, we will focus on two approaches, which adhere to the traditional ideal of non-directiveness, but qualify this ideal in an important way.

Firstly, the so-called '(moral) education' model of non-directive counselling, developed by the American philosopher John Arras (1990). This model is based upon a distinction between autonomy as the client's right of final decision making, which it respects, and absolute autonomy in the process of deciding, which it rejects. Although the counsellor would not tell the client what to do, and although he would respect the final decision of the client, he would attempt to confront the client with the moral dilemmas the client actually faces. So this model allows the counsellor to direct the client through a value-based scrutiny of the available options, playing an active role in expanding the client's awareness of the moral issues posed.

Activity:

Make a list of the pros and cons of the moral education model of genetic counselling before reading the following comment of Guido de Wert (1999b).

The 'moral education' model of counselling need not threaten reproductive autonomy. It may even increase reproductive autonomy by contributing to genuinely informed decision making. Nevertheless, this model raises some questions that need further scrutiny. What, for instance, about the risk that this model entails de facto 'covert prescriptions'? Clearly, there is a fine line between moral education on the one hand and recommending a specific decision on the other hand. Furthermore, because of practical constraints, the counsellor will not (always) be able to address all the ethical aspects and issues involved. If the counsellor chooses which of the normative questions should be addressed, which criteria will/should he use for this selection? Is not there a serious risk that the moral span of the diverse options will be narrowed because of the particular moral beliefs of the individual counsellor? Finally, it is important to realise that discussion on the part of the counsellor has the potential to function as coercion in the life of the client (Yarborough 1989). After all, the psychological dynamics of the clinical setting can undermine the equality between client and counsellor.

Activity:

Looking at the pros and cons of the moral education model, do you think that this model can be morally justified? If so, how could this model be applied in the counselling of Tim and Marian (who have a 50 percent risk of having a child carrying the Huntington's disease mutation)?

The *second* example of a more differentiated way of thinking about (non-)directiveness can be found in the report of the Ethics Committee of the Royal Dutch Society of Physicians (1997). While this committee stresses the importance of non-directiveness, the commission at the same time acknowledges that there might be exceptions to the rule. In so-called 'extreme risk' situations, i.e., in situations where there is a high risk of devastating harm to the future child, the doctor might give his unsolicited opinion/advice. In view of the objections to and the risks of directiveness, the Commission stresses that directiveness can be allowed only in exceptional cases and on *some conditions*:

1. The counsellor should stress that he is giving his personal opinion.
2. He should try to influence the client only by rational (noncoercive) persuasion.
3. He should discuss these exceptional cases with his team, or ask for a second opinion (in order to avoid entirely subjective recommendations).

Activity:

Do you agree that there may be exceptions to the ideal of non-directive reproductive genetic counselling? In particular, do you think that giving unsolicited advice to prospective parents at risk of having an affected child may be justified in some cases? If not, why not? If so, do you support the conditions mentioned by the Ethics Committee?

Prenatal Testing and Selective Abortion

One of the options for preventing the birth of an affected child is prenatal diagnosis, followed by abortion in case of a 'positive' result. This type of abortion is termed 'selective' abortion. The main methods of prenatal diagnosis are the so-called chorionic villus sampling and amniocentesis.

Prenatal diagnosis is controversial. The arguments in favour of or against prenatal diagnosis come from different moral traditions. More generally, each moral tradition may suggest a perspective from which moral judgements concerning prenatal testing or other 'genetic technologies' may be justified. The box below presents a brief overview of the main ethical theories that are based on these traditions.

ETHICAL THEORY

Each moral tradition suggests a perspective from which moral judgements may be justified. Here we will use the distinction, quite common in philosophy, between *consequentialist* and *deontological* (or nonconsequentialist) theories. Essentially, the former is based on the assumption that what makes an action right is exclusively its consequences. The most important consequentialist theory is *utilitarianism*, which evaluates the consequences mainly in terms of the good produced by the action. The principle of utility states, in fact, that the right action is that which produces the highest good for the largest number of individuals involved. The latter is a group of various theories which propose that, whatever the consequences, certain kinds of moral considerations are paramount in the formulation of an ethical judgement. The difference between the various deontological theories depends on the basic assumptions which ground the moral considerations. Very sketchily, we may distinguish here between deontological theories which have a *metaphysical* basis (such as a metaphysical conception of human nature), *libertarian* theories, based on the primacy of the principle of autonomy (self-determination), and Kantian theories, based on the *Kantian* principle of respect for every human person as an end in itself.

● *Consequentialist* arguments imply that any practice which results in more welfare than another (e.g., eliminating defective genes from the human endowment) is preferable. Genetic testing, selecting characteristics of future children and, eventually, genetic therapy are acceptable provided that the foreseeable consequences are not disastrous for the persons involved (Singer and Wells 1984). Consequentialist authors usually criticise traditional views and premises. We have the responsibility for our future and for the destiny of future generations, and we should exercise control over the diffusion of genetic diseases in order to avoid worse consequences. Replacing nature as a guide of evolution is not so much an exercise of power as it is a form of responsibility.

Activity:

Stop and carefully consider this perspective: the acceptability of genetic testing and genetic intervention is based exclusively on the good and bad consequences produced. How would you qualify a good consequence in this field? Is this the only relevant criterion for these issues?

- *Deontological* arguments are of various kinds:
a) In some cases, this position is connected with theological premises concerning the conception of man as an image of God ('Imago Dei').

b) Libertarian authors have a totally different attitude, though still on deontological grounds: we should fully recognise individuals' rights to freedom, as long as they do not inflict serious harm upon others. The right to procreative freedom implies, amongst other things, that individuals (not only couples) may select the characteristics of their progeny and even choose to improve the genetic endowment of their children (Robertson 1994).

c) A third perspective would require that these practices never violate the respect we owe to any person as a rational being and therefore an end in themselves.

Activity:

Consider these arguments carefully. Are their premises necessary and sound? Are the arguments coherent and do they adhere to the common moral experience? Hold a short discussion on the arguments and the theories mentioned here and highlight their respective advantages and disadvantages.

Somewhat independently of the ethical theory adopted, there are some recurring arguments that are used in the debates on genetic technology. For example, it is very common in these debates that arguments are formulated in the typical format of the *slippery slope*. Usually, a *historical-sociological* version of the argument is used, rather than a purely *logical* one: even if some conceptual line may be drawn between, say, selective abortions for the purpose of preventing the birth of a seriously handicapped child on the one hand and selection for trivial reasons on the other, that line is so thin that we will not be able to stop the slipping of society as a whole towards unacceptable forms of eugenics. This kind of argument is of a consequentialist kind, but it is mainly used by deontologists in order to show that liberal policies may have unacceptable consequences.

The main argument in favour of prenatal diagnosis/selective abortion is that it may prevent serious harm to the child and/or the individual family. At the same time, prenatal diagnosis is controversial, mainly because of its link with abortion. The main objections come from the so-called 'foetalist' perspective, which focuses on the moral status of the foetus, and the 'disability rights' perspective. Let us very briefly review these objections/perspectives:

There is a considerable difference of opinion with regard to the moral status of the foetus. At one end of the spectrum lies the so-called 'conceptionalist' view (arguing that 'human personal life starts at fertilisation') and the 'strong' version of the potentiality argument: 'because of the potential of the foetus to develop into a person, the foetus ought to be respected and protected as a person'. According to these views, (selective) termination of pregnancy cannot be justified. On the other side of the spectrum we find the view that the foetus as a 'non-person' ought not to be attributed any moral status at all. As a consequence, (selective) abortion is perceived as a morally neutral, 'self-regarding' act. In between these extremes are other different positions. Here a kind of 'overlapping consensus' exists: the foetus deserves real, but relative, protection.

Many people think that abortion can be morally justified, if there are 'good reasons'. Preventing the birth of a seriously handicapped child may be one of these 'good' reasons. It is important to realise, however, that some commentators argue that *selective* abortions are ethically more problematic than 'traditional' *non*-selective abortions (i.e., termination of unwanted pregnancies). The 'disability rights' critique, for instance, argues that the practice of selective abortion is at odds with the interests of handicapped people.

Prenatal testing, and in particular selective abortion, are criticised from the disability rights perspective, as they conflict (according to this charge) with the rights and interests of disabled people. Among others, the following objections can be discerned:

- Selective abortion discriminates against the handicapped, and entails a denial of their equal worth and even their very right to exist.
- As the use of genetic technologies reduces the number of persons suffering from genetic disorders, public support for the disabled will dwindle (the so-called 'loss of support argument').

There is an ongoing debate about the validity and merits of the disability rights critique. One may argue that it is unwarranted to construe a conflict between, on the one hand, the needs and rights of prospective parents who want to decrease their risk of having a handicapped child and, on the other hand, the interests of disabled people. In response to the first objection, Chadwick (1987) states that it is not only *handicapped* foetuses that are aborted. Thousands of healthy foetuses are also aborted, for example if they constitute a threat to the health or welfare of the mother. But this does not lead to the view that any adult that is a threat to someone's health or welfare is less worthy of respect. The important boundary here is that between foetuses and adults, not between handicapped and healthy.

The 'loss of support argument' is controversial too. Firstly, those who advance this objection do not provide empirical data to support it. Furthermore, even if there did turn out to be some loss of support for certain genetic diseases as their incidence declines, it would not follow that seeking to reduce their incidence is wrong, all things considered. Clearly there is a social obligation to maintain – and even to improve – support for disabled people, but this does not generate a claim on the part of those individuals that society must ensure that their numbers do not decrease (Buchanan et al. 2000).

Activity:

Before moving further, stop here for a few moments and try to link the 'fetalist' and 'disability rights' objections to the ethical theories presented in the box above. Would you qualify these objections as deontological, consequentialist, or 'mixed'? In addition, formulate your own position regarding the status of the foetus and the disability rights critique.

We will now concentrate on some ethical problems regarding the prospective parents' (mothers') right *not* to know and the right to know.

The (prospective) parents' right not to know

The issue of the prospective parents' right *not* to know was introduced in an intriguing case presented by Carmen Rauch:

The case of Emily and Martin

Emily and Martin came for prenatal diagnosis. Emily was thirty-nine years old. The couple was principally concerned about Down's syndrome. When the test was ready, the clinical geneticist invited the couple in to discuss the results. 'We haven't detected Down's syndrome, but we did find another little problem – your son has Klinefelter's syndrome'. 'What's that?' Emily and Martin asked. 'You see, your son will be quite normal until puberty. Then he will become rather tall, which isn't really a problem. But he will have a tendency to be fat, especially on the upper part of his body, he will have a very small penis and small testicles, and he will be sterile. Otherwise there are no special features.' Emily and Martin went back home, very disturbed. They became preoccupied with encyclopaedias and the Internet. They decided to carry the pregnancy to term, but they wrote an angry letter to the clinical geneticist. 'Now we see our son as a Klinefelter's case. We saw so many pictures showing what a Klinefelter's case looks like and we cannot forget those pictures! We could have had so many years without any problem, but now we know ... We would have preferred not to know!'

A first comment is provided by Louis Archer

For the discussion of this case we may identify, at least, the following ethical issues: the conditions for appropriate genetic counselling, and the right (not) to know.

One of the conditions for sound genetic counselling is that the problem under consideration is clearly defined. In the case of prenatal diagnosis, the future parents should be led to state exactly what kind of genetic diagnosis they want. If they ask to be informed about any genetic anomaly detectable by the technique used, a longer discussion with and preparation of the couple should take place. Extensive information should be given about the different anomalies, together with a discussion of the pros and cons of knowing or not knowing. By imagining the theoretical possibility of a disease which is not declared before puberty, the couple would have to decide whether they preferred to be prepared for it ahead of time or not.

If, on the contrary, their question was just about Down's syndrome, only the negative result should be communicated to them, and not the finding concerning Klinefelter's syndrome. Clearly, the right not to know should be exercised in full awareness of the risks connected with not knowing.

In the current case, the couple complains about being informed about something they would have preferred not to know. If the Klinefelter's syndrome were simply omitted in the report of the diagnosis, the parents could later complain that the prenatal diagnosis was not truthful, incomplete, and didn't prepare them psychologically for the real situation. In the initial counselling all this should have been taken into account in order to produce an informed decision by Emily and Martin regarding the results to be obtained by prenatal testing.

A second comment comes from Piers Benn

This apparently simple case raises many questions about the value of advance knowledge of an undesirable condition, about parents' rights to such knowledge, about the future welfare of both the son and his parents and, indirectly, about the moral acceptability of abortion after genetic testing has revealed abnormalities of various kinds. The central issue, though, seems to be that of disclosure, including both proper communication skills and proper balancing of interests when deciding whether to disclose facts that have not been specifically enquired about.

Did the geneticist do the parents a service, a disservice, or neither, when s/he revealed the result of the test, bearing in mind that the test was for Down's syndrome, which the couple would have wanted disclosed, but not for anything else? The parents wished they had not been told, and clearly felt afterwards that the geneticist was wrong to give the information and has in some sense harmed them by doing so. But this alone does not show that the geneticist acted unreasonably. The geneticist probably encounters many other parents who do want to know such things. These parents would be very angry if such information were withheld, and highly resentful of the seemingly paternalistic attitude to them that this would show. Moreover, some people are adept at changing their minds while claiming to have been consistent all along, one day not wanting information and later blaming doctors for not having giving them the information. Geneticists and other bearers of 'explosive' information will often feel that whether or not they do the right thing is a matter of luck.

At the same time, it does not look as though the case was handled with due sensitivity or care. There are ways of finding out whether a patient, or parent, wishes to know certain things. Doctors, in particular those who work in palliative care, learn ways of sensing how much people wish to be told about their condition. Naturally it is hard to do this without prematurely arousing parents' suspicions that there is an alarming diagnosis or prognosis, but good communication skills can help a great deal.

There are other more general questions about advance knowledge. Suppose that the parents have both a right to know and a right not to know whether their future child will suffer from a genetic abnormality. We might argue that the parents' right not to know had been violated in this case, since they were not asked whether they wanted to be given further information. But the moral questions raised by such fore-knowledge are not only about rights. For you can harm people without violating their rights and you can violate people's rights without harming them. The parents' lives, and possibly the child's as well, may be damaged by the advance knowledge of the onset of Klinefelter's syndrome. 'Ignorance is bliss', as the saying has it. On the other hand, optimists will argue that ignorance is far from bliss in this case, since advance knowledge will help the parents, and perhaps even the child, to prepare for the onset of the condition. Whether this is correct is largely an empirical matter. There are good things to say on either side.

Activity:

Make a comparison of the views of Archer and Benn and try to identify the major difference(s). If you feel sympathy for Archer's view, try to make your justification of this view as strong as possible by integrating a rebuttal of Benn's counterargument(s) – and vice versa.

The (prospective) parents' right to know

Do prospective parents have the right to get information about the (medical) condition of the unborn child? If so, what is the scope of this right? Is this right absolute or not?

Looking more closely, various related questions can be discerned. Below, we will focus on just two of these. Firstly, in view of the debate over the morality of abortion, should the indications for prenatal diagnosis be restricted, and if so, how? Secondly, is it morally justified for counsellors to refuse prenatal diagnosis in cases where women are unwilling to consider terminating the pregnancy in the case of an unfavourable test result?

A. Indications for prenatal diagnosis: the case of late(r) onset disorders

The criteria/indications for prenatal diagnosis is a topical issue. Some people argue for restrictive criteria, in view of the 'moral value' of unborn human life. They consider restrictions to be crucial in order to prevent a (further) 'trivialisation' of abortion. Others consider flexible guidelines, which allow for consideration of individual cases, to be of the utmost importance. Prenatal diagnosis for 'late(r) onset' disorders, which manifest themselves later in life, is particularly controversial. In some countries, selective abortion is not (or may not be) legally allowed in these cases. Even if it was legally accepted, some people argue that aborting a foetus which carries a predisposition for a late onset disorder is wrong from a moral point of view.

Below we will present firstly, prenatal testing for late onset *untreatable* disorders, and secondly, prenatal diagnosis for late onset disorders which may be *treatable*.

Late onset untreatable disorders

Huntington's disease is the paradigm case for this category (even though only a small minority of people at risk for Huntington's disease opt for prenatal testing).

The case of Tim and Marian

After extensive deliberations, Marian and Tim finally opt for prenatal diagnosis, because they want to prevent giving birth to a child carrying the Huntington's mutation.

Activity:

Make a list of moral arguments for and against prenatal diagnosis aimed at preventing the birth of a carrier of Huntington's disease. Do you think that this option can be morally justified? Why (not)? We will ask you to reflect on these questions again after reading the views of Stephen Post and Guido de Wert:

Aborting a foetus carrying the Huntington's disease mutation has been most explicitly criticised by the American philosopher Stephen Post (1991). The child, so he argues, will have many decades of good and unimpaired living. Moreover, the parents of the child are not immediately or even directly affected in the way they would be were the disease of early onset. Post's reservations about prenatal testing for Huntington's disease are based on two humanistic considerations: firstly, our desire not to bring suffering into the world must be tempered by the recognition that suffering is a part of life, and escapes human prevention to a large degree. Technology may prevent our coming to grips with the basic existential reality of contingency from which we never fully escape. Secondly, we should acknowledge the moral ambiguity of the quest for 'perfect' babies ('perfectionism'), and resist 'the tyranny of the normal'. People who are different and 'imperfect' teach us about the meaning of equality and commitment. We must, according to Post, be highly circumspect about declaring too imperfect those persons who must endure somewhat earlier in life the very sorts of frailties that eventually assault each one of us.

Guido de Wert takes a different position. 'Of course, it would be a naïve and misguided effort to fight against all the contingencies of human life. The question is, however, whether carriers of Huntington's disease, who have a high (50 percent) risk of transmitting the mutation to their children, have the moral right to prevent this by making use of prenatal diagnosis and selective abortion. In view of the fact that Huntington's disease is a severe disease, and that the penetrance of the mutation is complete, my answer is yes. It is insensitive, if not an insult, to disqualify preventive measures as symptomatic of 'genetic perfectionism'. Of course, carriers of Huntington's disease will be healthy during three to four decades. One needs to recognise, however, that the prospect of their eventual fate often imposes an extremely severe burden. The objection that carriers of Huntington's disease 'endure just somewhat earlier in life the frailties that eventually assault each one of us' is misplaced. This objection might be valid, however, with regard to prenatal testing for the late onset version of Alzheimer's disease, which has a substantially later onset than Huntington's disease. Personally, I was deeply impressed by the desperate sigh of the widow of a Huntington's disease patient: "When my husband died after twenty-five years of illness, I felt like a light had finally come on at the end of the tunnel. Now I watch my daughter and see her movements and the light has extinguished." Apparently, Post completely ignores the perspective of the healthy relatives.'

Activity:
Compare your list of 'pros and cons' regarding prenatal diagnosis of Huntington's disease, as well as your personal moral view, with the opinions of both of these commentators. Do you think that, all things considered, aborting a carrier of Huntington's disease can be morally justified? Did you change your mind after reading the commentaries? If so, why?

Late onset disorders which may be treatable
A good example is hereditary breast/ovarian cancer (see box below for some background information). To begin with, it should be noted that members of affected families have until now shown hardly any interest in prenatal testing for these disorders. This should be no surprise in view of the clinical experience with prenatal testing for Huntington's disease. Nevertheless, the ethics of such applications need debate.

Hereditary breast and ovarian cancer

Breast and ovarian cancer both result from genetic and environmental factors leading to the accumulation of mutations in essential genes. The most widely accepted model of breast and ovarian cancer susceptibility is that they are due to a small number of highly penetrant mutations (such as in the genes termed BRCA 1 and BRCA2) and a much larger number of low-penetrance gene variants. Interaction between these genetic variants and environmental exposures is also important. Women with a BRCA1 or BRCA 2 mutation have a lifetime breast cancer risk of 50–85 percent. The median age of diagnosis of breast cancer in mutation carriers is forty-two years, more than twenty years earlier than the median for unselected women. Lifetime ovarian cancer risks of women carrying a BRCA 1 or BRCA 2 mutation are estimated at 10–65 percent. Men carrying a mutation in BRCA2 have an estimated 6 percent lifetime risk of breast cancer.

Female carriers can opt for preventive measures like regular mammography and preventive surgery (including mastectomy). The protective value of these measures for carriers has yet to be definitely established.

The ethics of prenatal testing for BRCA mutations was one of the topics in papers by Kris Dierickx and Guido de Wert

Kris Dierickx's commentary runs as follows: 'Proponents of providing a prenatal test for hereditary breast cancer state that in a pluralist society, this type of testing as well as abortion of a female carrier foetus should be allowed. Furthermore, a society which allows abortion for many social reasons should not prohibit this type of abortion. It is, according to the proponents, important to realise that BRCA mutations have a high penetrance, and that the preventive and therapeutic measures are limited. Clearly, genetic counselling and psychological support are indispensable in the preparation for eventual prenatal tests. Maximising the autonomy of the women concerned, with the aim of permitting them to make free and informed decisions, is to be preferred to a legal prohibition of prenatal BRCA mutation testing. Some proponents, however, add that only if sex determination shows a female foetus should testing for BRCA mutation be performed. Opponents of prenatal testing for BRCA mutations argue, however, that BRCA mutation carriers born today will probably be able to avail themselves of dramatically improved preventive measures, as well as tumour diagnosis and therapy, 20–30 years from now.'

According to Guido de Wert, 'Prenatal testing for BRCA mutations is more controversial then prenatal testing for Huntington's disease. After all, the penetrance of these mutations is incomplete, and preventive interventions like regular mammography and prophylactic mastectomy may effectively reduce morbidity and mortality in carriers. We should resist, however, premature conclusions with regard to preventing the birth of (female) foetuses predisposed to hereditary breast and ovarian cancer. Morally relevant questions concern:

a) the effectiveness of available preventive and/or therapeutic measures, and

b) the burden imposed by the respective medical interventions.

Certainly the effectiveness of mammography seems currently to be far from optimal. It is hoped that the inclusion of magnetic resonance imaging in screening examinations will allow earlier detection of breast cancer in these women, and result in a lower mortality rate (Tilanus-Linthorst et al. 2000). A recent study suggests that the effectiveness of preventive mastectomy may be high, but longer follow-up and study of more patients is necessary to definitely establish the protective effect (and determine the long-term complications) of this procedure (Meijers-Heijboer et al., 2001). Clearly, prophylactic surgery is irreversible, and may have major implications for these women's quality of life.

In view of these residual risks and burdens, I would argue that the fear of prospective ('at risk') parents that their future daughter(s) may inherit a BRCA gene mutation is far from unreasonable, and that prevention of the birth of daughters strongly predisposed to hereditary breast and ovarian cancer is not a trivial concern. I assume, for the moment, that future requests for prenatal diagnosis of BRCA gene mutations will primarily come from members of severely affected families. In these cases, the penetrance of the BRCA-gene mutations will probably be highest, and performing prenatal diagnosis least problematic from a moral point of view.'

Activity:

What do you think of these arguments? What, according to you, is the moral weight of the 'slippery slope' argument? Do you think that if we accept prenatal diagnosis of mutations in breast/ovarian cancer genes and the abortion of female foetuses carrying one of these mutations, that prenatal testing and selective abortion will be performed *for ever less weighty reasons* – and that this is a good reason to prohibit prenatal testing for breast/ovarian cancer mutations?

B. Prenatal diagnosis: only for women considering abortion?

The case of Monique

Monique, thirty-eight years old, requests prenatal diagnosis for Down's syndrome. She is not prepared to terminate the pregnancy in the case of an unfavourable result. Her main reason for

> applying for the test is that she wants to prepare herself for the birth of a handicapped child.

Opinions differ as to whether prenatal testing should be available for women who are not willing to consider termination of pregnancy, irrespective of the test result. The main objections are:

- Since testing is expensive and facilities are scarce, priority for the use of prenatal diagnosis should be given to women who intend to terminate pregnancy in the case of an unfavourable test result.
- Being informed that the foetus has an abnormality will be a heavy burden for those who will not accept an abortion.
- The tests themselves are not risk-free; even if done in specialised centres, invasive prenatal diagnosis results in miscarriage in 0.5–1.0 percent of the cases.

The dominant view in ethics, however, is that women who have a medical indication for prenatal diagnosis should have 'unconditional' access to the test. Arguments include:

- They have the right to information about the health of the foetus.
- Reassurance as such is a positive outcome of the testing.
- Receiving a 'positive' result of the test may help prospective parents to prepare (psychologically and practically) for the birth of an affected child.

Activity:

What do you think of these arguments 'pro and con' limiting access to prenatal diagnosis to women who are prepared to consider termination of pregnancy? Do you feel that there are any additional arguments? One could, for instance, argue that to limit access to prenatal diagnosis is at odds with the main goal of reproductive genetic counselling (cf. the section 'Reproductive Autonomy and the Ideal of Non-directive Councelling').

The case of Patricia

Tim's sister Patricia is also a carrier of Huntington's disease. Like Tim and Marian, Patricia and her partner, Harold, eventually decide to apply for prenatal testing. Their main reason is, however, that they want to be reassured. Termination of pregnancy is, so they tell the counsellor, completely unacceptable to them.

Activity:

Make a comparison between the case of Monique and the case of Patricia. Are these cases similar from a moral point of view? Or are there any morally relevant differences? Try to formulate your view. We will come back to this case in the next chapter.

Preimplantation Genetic Diagnosis

An alternative for prenatal testing may be preimplantation genetic diagnosis (PGD), i.e., testing embryos in vitro, prior to implantation, aiming at a selective transfer (box below).

Preimplantation Genetic Diagnosis

PGD is a method intended to detect gene mutations or chromosomal aberrations in the embryo in vitro. PGD involves various stages. Firstly, in vitro fertilisation or intracytoplasmic sperm injection (a variant of in vitro fertilisation, whereby one single sperm is injected directly into the egg). Secondly, the biopsy of one or two cells from the embryo. Third, the genetic analysis of these cells (PGD in the strict sense), aiming at, fourth, a selective transfer of the 'unaffected' embryo(s).

PGD allows a woman/couple at high risk of having a child affected by a specific disorder to begin a pregnancy knowing right from the start that the child will not suffer from this disorder. The selective transfer eliminates (or at least strongly reduces) the need to consider a selective abortion. Most women/couples opting for PGD have objections to prenatal testing/selective abortion, have a burdensome reproductive history or are subfertile, and apply for in vitro fertilisation primarily for that reason.

Due to the technical complexities of single cell diagnosis, the actual potential of PGD is still limited. PGD is still experimental. The moderate success rate as well as the costs of in vitro fertilisation deter widespread adoption of this strategy.

PGD is the subject of disagreement as to its acceptability. There are arguments both in favour and against. The (main) issue at the base of these discussions concerns the status of, and the kind of respect due to, human preimplantation embryos. The polar opposition we find concerning the 'moral value' of foetuses is mirrored here (cf. the section 'Prenatal Testing and Selective Abortion'). Even the terms used in this discussion are not neutral. Some publications use the term 'pre-embryo' to indicate the human embryo before implantation and the development of the primitive streak, i.e., the authors apparently assume that a pre-embryo deserves less respect than a more developed embryo, a foetus, a newborn, a child or an adult. This is not commonly agreed language; it implies some theoretical and normative assumptions which are controversial. Working on the issues covered by this paragraph, you will inevitably meet these fundamental issues, knowing that there is at the moment no general consensus on them and that everyone needs to argue his or her position in the different contexts with the best arguments available.

While most countries allow PGD on some conditions, some countries, including Germany, prohibit PGD altogether (Embryo Protection Act 1990). The following case (dedicated to Prof. Volker von Loewenich, neonatologist, Frankfurt am Main) illustrates some of the problems that may arise from this lack of harmony between various nations.

The case of Peter and Karin

Peter and Karin are very happy with their first baby. However, after a few weeks they notice that the baby's movements seem to be decreasing. The paediatrician refers the child to the hospital immediately. Soon after, Peter and Karin learn that their child almost certainly is affected by a muscle disease with an extremely poor prognosis: Werdnig-Hoffmann syndrome (spinal muscular atrophy).

The baby's condition deteriorates rapidly; the desperate parents are informed about 'specimens being stored for future use'. As they are so concerned with their dying child, they do not grasp the meaning of 'future' use.

A few months after the child has died, Karin becomes pregnant again. The obstetrician refers the couple to a geneticist, as they have asked for advice concerning the possibility of prenatal diagnosis. From the geneticist they learn that prenatal diagnosis is possible, a time-consuming analysis of the stored material from the first child being necessary however. Werdnig-Hoffmann syndrome is now confirmed by DNA analysis of the specimen from the first child, and unfortunately prenatal diagnosis also reveals the expected child to be affected. Peter and Karin decide to have the pregnancy terminated.

As they are desperately longing for an unaffected child, they seek counselling again. Discussing reproductive options, they reject the idea of adoption. The counsellor informs them that ovum donation is not allowed in Germany and that artificial insemination by donor is only available to married couples. Very moved by the sad story of the two children that Peter and Karin already lost, the counsellor discusses the case with her colleagues and they decide to suggest the couple should consider the option of PGD. This necessarily has to be carried out abroad and Peter and Karin will have to pay for the procedure themselves. To them, however, this seems the only acceptable option and they arrange for an appointment at Brussels University Hospital.

Activity:

Discuss the case, focusing first on the reasons the couple has to opt for PGD in their case. Consider motives in favour, motives against and possible alternative courses of action. A second issue here is the problem of whether or not to legally allow PGD. In case of a legal prohibition, those citizens who wish to have PGD in any case will have to go abroad, to a country where PGD is allowed. On the other side, there is the problem of legalising a practice when there is no consensus among citizens and deep values are at stake.

In her commentary, Jeantine Lunshof goes into three issues concerned with the role of the medical profession and the extent of professional beneficence:
1) Should genetic/reproductive information be given without formal request?

One of the tragic aspects of the case is the pregnancy with an affected foetus so shortly after the first child had died. Obviously counselling concerning genetic aspects and recurrence risk did not take place. The case describes the parents as being fully preoccupied with caring for their dying child; they obviously did not ask for more information, even as they were told about specimens being taken for 'future use'. Given the fact that a new pregnancy not infrequently occurs shortly after parents have lost a child, we must ask whether highly relevant information like a recurrence risk of 25 percent should actively be offered to a couple, even without request for counselling. Karin and Peter were, on the one hand, not burdened with information they might not have wished to have, but on the other hand they did not have the opportunity to make an informed reproductive decision.

2) Moral obligations versus legal prohibitions
The case takes place in Germany, where the Embryo Protection Act (1990) forbids manipulating embryos, including PGD. Opinions concerning the issue are, however, in society at large as well as among the medical profession, highly divided. In a case like the one at hand, the only way to have an unaffected child that is biologically one's own – without taking the chance of facing the dilemma of selective abortion – is by PGD. Should a physician/counsellor discuss with parents/clients an option that is illegal (in his own country)? Does the individual duty of professional beneficence outweigh the medical association's selective self-binding in supporting the current law? If a couple decides that PGD is the only acceptable option to them (morally as well as psychologically), should the counsellor offer help in acting upon their decision? In Germany, giving advice concerning the option of PGD abroad seems not to be punishable. The question, therefore, is more concerned with the limits of professional beneficence.

3) A professional obligation: good collegiality across the border.
Usually patients are referred to colleagues abroad because diagnostic or therapeutic facilities are for scientific, technical or financial reasons not available in their own country. In the current case, a diagnostic procedure, PGD, is not available because it is against the law and besides that is considered to

be immoral by many, including many members of the medical profession. The referral is not because of higher technical, but because of (implicitly assumed) 'lower' (more permissive) moral standards.

More restrictive indications for PGD than for prenatal diagnosis?

It is sometimes argued that the indications for PGD should be more restrictive than the indications accepted for regular prenatal diagnosis (during pregnancy). A Dutch committee, for instance, recommended that PGD should (for the moment) be performed only for 'severe, untreatable' disorders (Core Committee 1993). As a consequence, PGD would not be allowed for disorders like haemophilia. The Ethics Committee of the German 'Gesell/schaft für Humangenetik' – to give a second example – suggested allowing PGD in the case of a 'serious childhood disorder or developmental defect' ('schwerwiegende kindliche Erkrankung oder Entwicklungsstörung') (Society for Human Genetics 1996). Following this guideline, PGD should not be performed for later onset disorders.

Guido de Wert (1999a) presented the following commentary

From an ethical point of view, it would be difficult to justify a priori stricter indications for PGD than for regular prenatal diagnosis. After all, a preimplantation embryo does not have a 'higher' moral status than a foetus – accordingly, a selective transfer is not more difficult to justify than a selective abortion. Imposing stricter indications for PGD might, however, be justified on the basis of (more or less) contingent consid-erations. Let me briefly review (some of) these arguments:

a. 'PGD involves a heavy burden, especially for the woman'.

This argument is unjustifiably paternalistic. After all, women should be enabled to balance the pros and cons of the various options themselves, and then make their own decision. Furthermore, the paternalistic objection hardly applies to *infertile* couples at high genetic risk, who opt for IVF to treat their infertility.

b. 'The reliability of the tests is unproven.'

I presume that the underlying fear concerns (the small but real) risk of false-negative test results, resulting in an affected pregnancy or even in the birth of an affected child. Even if the experimental nature of the test should be regarded (for the moment) as a valid reason to 'set limits' (although at least some of the tests used are currently highly reliable in experi-enced hands), the conclusion that PGD should be performed only for serious, untreatable disorders is debatable. After all, the potential burden imposed by a false-negative result would be less if the condition is mild or treatable.

c. 'The experimental biopsy carries unknown risks to the health of the future child.'

This argument has become less convincing as clinical experi-ence up to now suggests that the biopsy carries no such risk. A systematic anomaly assessment should provide further data (Simpson and Liebaers 1996).

d. 'PGD involves an additional loss of embryos'.

One might argue, firstly, that as isolated blastomeres are totipotent, i.e., have the capacity to develop into a complete individual, these cells have the same moral status as embryos. For some critics, this is a strong reason to argue that the destruction of these 'cells' in the diagnostic process is morally unjustified. The presumed totipotency of individual blas-tomeres at the six to ten cell stage is, however, unlikely (McLaren 1997). A second version of this argument concerns the unintended loss of embryos as a consequence of 'biopsy failure'. According to the experts, however, such embryo loss rarely happens in experienced hands.

Summarising, it may be concluded that the arguments in favour of more restrictive indications for PGD are either logically incoherent or, in view of the clinical experience, weak. Defects or disorders that are 'serious enough' to qualify for prenatal diagnosis should also qualify for PGD.

Activity:

Would you qualify the arguments in favour of more restrictive indications for PGD as deontological, consequentialist, or 'mixed? Further, do you consider De Wert's rebuttal of these arguments to be convincing? Try to evaluate the argument that 'PGD involves an additional loss of embryos' from the various positions regarding the moral status of the embryo (cf. the section 'Prenatal Testing and Selective Abortion'). Do you think that people's view of the validity of this argument at least partly depends on their view of the status of the embryo?

Less restrictive indications?

Maybe the real ethical question is not whether the indications for PGD should be *more* restrictive than the indications for regular prenatal diagnosis, but whether the indications for PGD could be *less* restrictive. After all, many consider preimplantation embryos to have a lower moral status than foetuses. Accordingly, one might argue that selection of preimplantation embryos on the basis of less serious grounds could be justified.

Activity:

Do you think that it makes a moral difference whether it is abortion or nonimplantation that we are considering? It is clear that an issue here is whether preimplantation embryos somehow deserve less protection than foetuses and children: is there a *graduality* in the moral value of the different stages of human prenatal life? Why (not)?

The paradigm case of PGD for 'less serious' (some would say trivial) reasons is PGD for sex selection for social (nonmedical) reasons. The American lawyer/ethicist John Robertson (1992) takes a permissive position. He argues that 'screening out embryos on the basis of gender may be less clearly unethical than initially thought. The ethics of choosing the sex of offspring depends very much on the means employed. Abortion for sex selection is very different from preconception sperm separation selection techniques. Embryo selection on the basis of sex seems much closer to preconception techniques than to abortion.' More generally, Robertson takes the libertarian perspective, arguing that prospective parents may select the characteristics of their children ('Ethical Theory' box).

Activity:

Before reading further, stop here for a few moments and make a list of (potential) objections to PGD for sex selection for social reasons. Discern deontological objections on the one hand and consequentialist objections on the other hand.

The ethics of sex selection is complex. Critics argue, first, that sex selection (for nonmedical reasons) is inherently sexist. Others do not agree; they admit that people *may* have sexist reasons for sex selection, but that this need not be so. Sex selection, so they argue, might be used for 'balancing'; if people already have two sons, they might use this technique to conceive a daughter. A second objection is that sex selection will result in a serious disturbance of the so-called 'sex ratio', as most people will opt for boys. This risk may, indeed, be great in specific countries, like India or China, where many prospective parents have a strong preference for sons, but not in other countries, where this preference is much weaker or even absent. A third objection concerns the moral status of the embryo. Even if one agrees that the earlier the selection, the less ethically problematic it is, one could argue that destroying preimplantation embryos for sex selection purposes is at odds with the moral status of the embryo. Sex selection in the context of PGD (for social reasons) could, according to some of its proponents, take place *without* discarding preimplantation embryos of the undesired sex, by donating these embryos to infertile couples (a strategy called 'gender distribution') (Seibel et al. 1994). One may wonder, however, whether such donations would only add to the large numbers of frozen spare embryos waiting for adoptive parents. A related, fourth objection is that in the event that the transfer of the embryos of the desired sex does not result in an on-going pregnancy, one has to start a new IVF treatment while there are still 'healthy' embryos available for transfer. Can such a practice be justified, given the costs and the medical risks of additional in vitro fertilisation and PGD? A fifth objection concerns the *'slippery slope'*: sex selection for nonmedical reasons can set a precedent for 'positive eugenics', i.e., selection for nondisease characteristics, like intelligence, body build, etc. Positive eugenics may confer advantages upon the offspring, in particular the offspring of the economically advantaged, who can afford the costs of such testing. In view of this, Carson Strong concludes that we would at least need a greater confidence that the benefits would outweigh the harms before we would be ethically justified in proceeding with embryo selection for nonmedical reasons (Strong 1997).

Activity:

How do you evaluate these arguments for and against PGD aiming at sex selection for non-medical reasons? If you do object to this use of PGD, which argument(s) is (are) overriding?

Nondisclosure preimplantation genetic diagnosis

Recently, some investigators have suggested a new approach concerning PGD for (untreatable) late onset disorders, aimed at preserving the right not to know of 'at risk' parents and, at the same time, at avoiding the birth of a diseased child (Schulman et al. 1996). Let us call this approach 'nondisclosure' PGD. The box below presents some background information about this strategy.

Non-disclosure preimplantation genetic diagnosis

Genetic testing for serious, untreatable, dominantly inherited disorders, like Huntington's disease, is an example of the difficult dilemmas that genetic testing can raise. In this situation, the desire of clients to avoid transmission of a genetic disease may conflict with and be completely extinguished by the adverse effects of presymptomatic diagnosis of the at-risk parent. In practice, only a minority (10–20 percent) of individuals at risk apply for presymptomatic Huntington's disease testing. As a consequence, so the proponents of the current alternative argue, the potential of antenatal diagnosis to reduce the burden of genetic disease in the population, as well as the tragedy of recurrent cases within a family, is seldom realised. PGD now provides an approach in which antenatal testing can be offered without the adverse effects of presymptomatic diagnosis. Couples at risk could be offered PGD without ever being informed of the specific test results. The couples would be told only that embryos were formed and tested, and that only apparently disease-free embryos were replaced. The parents would specifically not be given any information about the number of eggs obtained, the number of embryos formed, the number in which diagnosis is successful, etc. In other words, no information would be given which might provide a basis for inferring whether or not any embryos with the Huntington's disease gene were ever identified. Hence, parents would derive no direct or indirect information about their own genetic risk, while PGD, if performed accurately, could reduce the foetal risk to zero.

What about the ethics of nondisclosure PGD?

Activity:

Before reading the comments of Guido de Wert and Roberto Mordacci, list a number of arguments for and against this practice. Then, critically contrast your opinion with those of the two commentators.

Guido de Wert comments as follows

Assuming that:
a) there are no overriding moral objections to in vitro fertilisation/PGD as such,
b) that individuals at risk of Huntington's disease do not have a moral duty 'to know', i.e., to apply for presymptomatic testing, and
c) that PGD for the Huntington's disease mutation can reliably be performed,

I restrict myself to some comments regarding the specific moral (morally relevant) aspects of *nondisclosure* PGD.

Firstly, the authors stress the public health implications of this approach: 'Perhaps it is not too early to consider the elimination of Huntington's disease and other extremely deleterious dominant disorders as a goal for the twenty-first century.' This eugenic perspective seems to be at odds with the (dominant) ethics of clinical genetics, which, indeed, give priority to the principle of respect for autonomy and to promoting informed reproductive decision making. Preventing the transmission of gene mutations may be the result of reproductive genetic counselling; it is not its (primary) goal. Anyway, aiming at the elimination of Huntington's disease is a 'mission impossible', in view of the occurrence of spontaneous mutations (dynamic triple repeats).

Secondly, nondisclosure testing as such raises troubling issues. The central question is, whether this approach can effectively protect the at-risk parent's preference not to know his/her own genetic status – and if it can, at what financial, medical and psychological cost? Let us suppose, for instance, that the first PGD cycle does not identify any carrier embryo. Depending on the exact number of embryos, the statistical risk of the parent at risk may become close to zero. To tell the client this good news would constitute an indirect and unintended breach of other at-risk clients' right not to know – after all, they may draw their own conclusions if they do not receive this good news. For this reason, I assume that one would withhold the good news. The problem, then, becomes, whether one should offer a second (and a third, fourth, etc.) in vitro fertilisation/PGD treatment, when the genetic risk has become almost nil.

Another problem arises when there are no embryos available for transfer in a given cycle, either because all the embryos are carriers of Huntington's disease, or for other reasons, like in vitro fertilisation failure. The client at risk might – rightly or wrongly – infer that he/she is a carrier. Should one consider a 'placebo transfer'?

Holding off on a definite stance with regard to nondisclosure PGD, I would still suggest: 'Das mag in der Theorie richtig sein, taugt aber nicht für die Praxis' (in theory, it may be a good approach, in practice, however, it is highly problematic).

Activity:

De Wert's reflections seem cautious as to the acceptability of nondisclosure PGD. Yet he offers a 'practical' argument based on the difficulties which this practice would face in maintaining its promises, i.e., protecting the right not to know of the parent at risk. In light of this argument, do you think nondisclosure PGD is feasible?

A different set of considerations emerges from the commentary of Roberto Mordacci

The practice of offering PGD to couples at risk of transmitting a genetic disease and withholding the information regarding the health status of the embryos thus produced raises serious problems.

In vitro fertilisation and PGD are offered here not as a treatment of infertility but as a form of preventive medicine. Actually, genetic defects are not really 'prevented' by this strategy; rather, defective embryos are prevented from being implanted and diseased children from being born. While utilitarians, denying the moral value of embryos, see nothing wrong with this, those deontologists who recognise the embryo as a person would reject this procedure as not showing due respect to persons.

The information that disease-free embryos are available seems necessary for the procedure to go on; the idea of a 'placebo' transfer sounds bizarre, considering that the procedure is rather invasive for the woman. Feminist writers would indisputably find such a proposal marked with unacceptable genderism. The information poses the problem that no good news means bad news, i.e., that one of the couple is a carrier and that no healthy embryo was detected. The right not to know of the couple would thus be violated. Yet rights theorists need not reject this possibility, since the violation of autonomy implicit in a placebo transfer is much more serious than the violation of the right not to know. All that is required is that the couple is informed beforehand that there is the possibility of finding no suitable embryo and that in this case the procedure should be repeated.

I would suggest that some virtue ethics theorists would probably find the attitude of couples who do not want to know lacking the virtue of courage: they are refusing to consider the perspective of a diseased child and, at the same time, rejecting the idea that some of their embryos may be defective even if these will not be implanted. They do not want to know about themselves, but this decision will have great consequences for their (possible) descendants. One should probably ask: why should I not want to know? Before deciding to try to become a parent, when there is this kind of risk, should one not be prepared, as a part of good character, to face reality and to assume the relevant responsibilities?

Activity:

What do you think of this argument? It seems that, in this direction, we should admit a 'duty to know' in cases where an individual has a risk of transmitting a genetic disease to his children. One may suggest that such a duty is based not on virtue ethics considerations, but on more explicitly deontological grounds, e.g., the duty to assume responsibility for one's own health, or even on consequentialist grounds, e.g., the duty to consider the consequences of procreating when there is a genetic risk. This duty would obviously be at odds with the statement of an absolute 'right not to know': what do you think about it? Can you imagine a way to harmonise this right with that duty?

This chapter addressed ethical questions and problems concerning *reproductive* genetic counselling and prenatal/preimplantation genetic diagnosis. The next chapter presents moral aspects of predictive genetic testing in healthy people, aiming at informing them about genetic risks for their future health.

Summary

In this chapter we have dealt with:
- the goals of reproductive genetic counselling and debates on the issue of 'nondirectiveness';
- the issue of selective abortion and the critique by the Disability Rights movement;

- the debate on the indications for prenatal diagnosis, in particular prenatal diagnosis of late onset disorders;
- the (possible) differences between the indications for prenatal diagnosis and preimplantation diagnosis.

We have analysed these issues by way of theoretical introductions and practical exercises, for example on responsible parenthood, the moral education model, the slippery slope argument, selective abortion and the possible dilemma between professional responsibility and the obligation to adhere to national laws.

Suggestions for further reading

Chadwick R.F. (ed.) (1987). *Ethics, Reproduction and Genetic Control*. London, New York: Routledge.

Davis DS. (2001). *Genetic Dilemmas: Reproductive Technology, Parental Choices, and Children's Futures*. New York, London: Routledge.

De Wert G. (2002). Ethical aspects of prenatal and preimplantation genetic testing for late-onset neurogenetic disease: the case of Huntington's disease. In *Prenatal testing of late onset neurogenetic disease*, G. Evers-Kiebooms, M. Zoeteweij and P. Harper, (eds), Oxford: BIOS, pp. 129–157.

Lamb D. (1988). *Down the slippery slope: Arguing in applied ethics*. London: Croom Helm.

Munthe C. (1999). *Pure selection: The ethics of preimplantation genetic diagnosis and choosing children without abortion*. Göteborg: Acta Universitatis Gothoburgensis.

Singer P. (ed.) (1991). *A Companion to Ethics. (Blackwell Companions to Philosophy)*. Oxford, Cambridge, MA: Blackwell.

- 2 -

Ethics of Predictive Genetic Testing

This chapter is concerned with the ethics of predictive genetic testing of adults as well as children ('minors'). Various types of predictive genetic testing are introduced in the first section. The second section presents ethical aspects and dilemmas of protocols to be used for predictive genetic testing.

Objectives

After reading this chapter you will be able to:

- understand the moral issues of predictive testing for genetic disorders.
- assess the difference between presymptomatic testing on the one hand and susceptibility testing for multifactorial disorders on the other hand.
- clarify the professional responsibilities of clinical geneticists regarding predictive testing for genetic disorders.
- create a protocol with principles and guidelines for predictive testing.
- evaluate from a moral viewpoint the various inclusion and exclusion criteria for predictive testing.
- identify and evaluate conflicting duties in the context of predictive testing caused by the familial nature of genetic information.

Introduction

The Human Genome Analysis project has resulted in the identification of many genes involved in human disorders, including late onset diseases, which manifest themselves later in life. These discoveries allow for so-called predictive DNA testing in asymptomatic ('healthy') individuals, in particular relatives of affected patients. The primary goal of this type of testing is to identify individuals at (very) high risk of developing the specific disorder. The certainty with which this prediction can be made depends largely upon the genetics of the specific condition. Autosomal dominant disorders may have a near complete penetrance, which means that the carrier of the genetic mutation involved will almost certainly develop the disorder. A good example is Huntington's disease. For so-called multifactorial disorders, which are caused by genetic as well as (mostly unknown) environmental factors, predictive testing could indicate a predisposition or susceptibility to the disorder. Whether the carrier of the susceptibility will develop the disorder is highly uncertain, as it depends upon environmental factors. Examples include common disorders like heart disease, (the late onset version of) Alzheimer's disease and diabetes. Predictive testing for autosomal dominant disorders is called *presymptomatic* testing, while predictive testing for multifactorial disorders is usually called *susceptibility* testing or *predispositional* testing. Clearly, these different types of disorders and of predictive genetic testing represent a spectrum, as the differences between them are more of degree than of substance.

There is an urgent need to analyse the ethical issues involved in predictive genetic testing. How can predictive genetic testing best be incorporated into health care? What is good clinical practice? This chapter concentrates on the cases of predictive testing for Huntington's disease and for hereditary cancers, in particular hereditary breast and ovarian cancer.

Ethical analysis

A preliminary moral question is whether it is morally justified to presymptomatically test for late onset disorders when effective preventive and/or therapeutic measures are not available (as for Huntington's disease) or highly speculative. There is no uniform answer to this question.

The case of Bob

Bob is a thirty-eight year-old professional musician. His mother suffers from Huntington's disease. The risk that Bob inherited the mutation is 50 percent. Bob wants to know his genetic status, and applies for the presymptomatic test. 'Knowing my genetic status,' he says, 'will help me to plan for the future'. The doctor, however, wonders whether it is good medical practice to perform predictive testing for untreatable lethal disorders – 'Why perform the test when we have nothing to offer to carriers?'

It is sometimes argued that presymptomatic diagnosis should be performed only when a therapeutic or prophylactic remedy is available or when an estimate of the risk of transmission can assist parents in making reproductive decisions: 'In other cases, predictive testing would conflict with the classical principle: first, do no harm'. Apparently, these critics consider the principle of respect for autonomy to be less important. Others hold that this position is too restrictive, for various reasons. First, this recommendation neglects that individuals at risk may have good reasons to apply for the test even if they do not plan to have a family and if therapeutic or prophylactic remedies are not available. Furthermore, for some persons at risk the uncertainty about their genetic status is unbearable. And third, experience with presymptomatic testing for Huntington's disease so far suggests that most clients can integrate the test result in their life. Obviously, this finding should be interpreted with caution. Indeed, this finding only applies to testees who received intensive pre and post-test counselling. Furthermore, the longterm effects of presymptomatic testing for Huntington's disease should be studied.

Activity:

What do you think of these arguments 'pro and con'? What would you do if you were Bob's doctor?

The case of Bob is an example of *presymptomatic* testing for autosomal dominant disorders. Similar questions arise when people ask for genetic *susceptibility* testing for untreatable disorders. The next case may illustrate the problems.

The case of Frances

Frances is fifty-two years old. Her father as well as one of her aunts suffer from the common type of Alzheimer's disease. When 'diagnostic' testing revealed that her father carries the genetic susceptibility, Frances became deeply concerned that she has inherited this susceptibility and that she will develop Alzheimer's disease too. She desperately wants to know whether she is 'at high risk' and applies for the predictive test. The doctor informs her that there is a strong international consensus not to perform this predictive test, for various reasons:

- the predictive value of this test is low; many carriers of the susceptibility will not develop Alzheimer's disease.
- there are no preventive or therapeutic measures available.
- the relevance of this type of information for reproductive decision making is highly questionable, if not completely absent, in view of both the (very) late onset of common Alzheimer's disease and the limited predictive value of the test.

Frances insists, however, that she wants to be tested, hoping that she will be reassured.

The genetics of Alzheimer's disease

Alzheimer's disease is a multifactorial disorder in a large majority of cases. Both genetic and environmental factors are relevant in the aetiology of the disease. The exact role of these factors in most cases of Alzheimer's disease is as yet unknown.

As to the genetic factors concerned, Alzheimer's disease is currently known to be associated with three 'causative' genes and at least 1 susceptibility trait. Mutations in one of these causative genes are autosomal dominant (like the Huntington's disease mutation) and pertain to early onset Alzheimer's disease with manifestations before the age of sixty-five. Approximately 90 percent of all Alzheimer's disease cases concern late onset Alzheimer's disease, which occurs after the age of sixty-five. Late onset Alzheimer's disease is associated with a susceptibility gene, termed ApoE-ε4. Carrying the susceptibility does not predict the onset of Alzheimer's disease, but accounts for an increased risk. In the near future, other causative genes and susceptibilities will undoubtedly be discovered.

> **Activity:**
>
> Make a brief comparison between presymptomatic testing for Huntington's disease on the one hand and susceptibility testing for Alzheimer's disease on the other hand. Do you think that these cases are similar from a moral point of view or that there are morally relevant differences? Explain your view.

A protocol

In view of the potential psychosocial risks of predictive genetic testing, it is considered important to use a protocol, to set a standard of 'good predictive testing practice'. A provisional protocol is sketched below, concentrating on the central ethical concerns and dilemmas.

> **Activity:**
>
> Stop here for a few moments, and try to sketch a protocol containing the main principles and guidelines for predictive testing. Please explain briefly why you consider these principles and guidelines to be important. Take into account both situations where adults want to be tested themselves and situations where parents request predictive testing for their young (incompetent) child.

The international guidelines for presymptomatic DNA diagnosis of Huntington's disease are used as a model (International Huntington Association and World Federation of Neurology 1994). An important question is which guidelines can be considered as 'universal', applicable to all cases of presymptomatic testing, and which guidelines are 'disease-specific'.

The text is based on papers by Kris Dierickx and Guido de Wert (De Wert 1998).

The protocol has four parts:
I.   Inclusion and exclusion criteria
II. Preparing for the test
III. Informing about the results of the test
IV. Post-test counselling and evaluation

This protocol concerns the ethics of *post*-natal testing only; the ethics of *pre*-natal testing for late onset disorders were addressed in Chapter 1.

I. Inclusion and exclusion criteria

Voluntariness

Clinical experience with presymptomatic testing for Hunting-ton's disease shows that external ('third party') pressure is a serious problem. Such pressure may take various forms. Firstly, pressure from family members, in particular partners or children. Secondly, pressure from professionals. In view of this experience, it must be anticipated that third party pres-sure can also arise in the context of predictive DNA testing for other disorders. Substantial control by third parties would make the consent given invalid. The principle of respect for autonomy implies that the counsellor has the responsibility to check whether the request for the test can be considered to be substantially voluntary.

> **Activity:**
>
> Clearly, a directive attitude (recommending a person at risk to have the presymptomatic test) is problematic when preventive or therapeutic measures which have proven efficacy are not yet avail-able (section IV of the protocol). But what if there is evidence that predictive testing and timely medical intervention can effectively prevent a serious disease? Would it still be unwarranted for the doctor to recommend to undergo predictive testing? Why (not)?

Competence

An adequate understanding of the implications of pre-symp-tomatic DNA-testing is a prerequisite for such testing.

If preventive/therapeutic remedies are not (yet) available or highly speculative, the question arises whether the doctor may refuse to give access to predictive testing for paternalistic reasons, i.e., on the basis of the 'best interests' of the client, and if so, on what conditions. Relevant in the ethical discussion is the distinction between *weak* and *strong* paternalism. Strong paternalism is the view that it can be right to interfere with a person's substantially autonomous decision for his own good. Weak paternalism holds that it can be right to interfere with a person's less-than-substantially autonomous decision making for his own good. Weak paternalism is not really controversial, because it involves no major violation of the principle of respect for autonomy; those whose wishes and preferences are overridden are acting with less than substantial autonomy. The issue of real controversy is strong paternalism. Some consider such paternalism (regarding substantially autonomous persons) to be justifiable too, on the condition that:

a) there is substantial evidence that otherwise the client will be in grave danger.
b) the overriding of the client's wish offers a reasonable prospect of bringing about a net benefit to him.
c) such overriding is the least restrictive way to achieve the desired protection (of his best interests) (DeGrazia 1991).

Critics of strong paternalism consider this guideline/policy to be unjustified, because it insufficiently respects the client's well-considered, subjective weighing of benefits and harms, risks and chances, of submitting to the test. Notwithstanding the latter controversy, it seems to be justified:

a) to offer (mandatory) pre-test 'psychological screening' as a condition for access to presymptomatic testing, given the importance of checking the applicant's capacity for autonomous decision making.
b) to postpone testing in case of significant doubt concerning an applicant's competence.

Activity:

While mandatory psychological screening may be justified as a means of protecting the applicant's autonomy, critics may argue that making this screening obligatory is anomalous, as it is at odds with the principle of respect for autonomy. What is your opinion?

While it is widely accepted that competence is a prerequisite for presymptomatic testing, one may wonder whether competence is absolutely essential in each and every case of presymptomatic testing. Take the following case:

The case of the Thompson family

Mr Thompson belongs to a family affected by hereditary breast and ovarian cancer. He is a carrier of a BRCA1 mutation. He and his wife worry that their twenty-eight year-old mentally retarded daughter Cynthia is a carrier too. They want, therefore, their daughter (an 'incompetent adult') to be tested for the BRCA1 mutation. If she proved to be a carrier, they would opt for regular monitoring/medical exams in order to reduce the risk for Cynthia.

Activity:

Do you think that testing Cynthia would be morally justified? How would you counsel the parents if they opted for preventive mastectomy instead of regular medical examinations?

Only adults – as a rule

A major issue is whether (healthy) minors may justifiably be tested for mutations for late(r) onset disorders, and, if so, on what conditions. At least two questions arise. Firstly, is it appropriate to presymptomatically test incompetent children at the request of their parents? And secondly, is it appropriate to test ('emancipated') minors who ask for such testing themselves? We will restrict ourselves to the first question.

There is a strong consensus that predictive testing of minors (at the request of the parents) for untreatable late onset disorders, like Huntington's disease, would be inappropriate, for at least two reasons (International Huntington Association and World Federation of Neurology 1994). First, the children's right not to know, i.e., their right to decide for themselves at some later stage whether or not to be presymptomatically tested, should be respected. Second, such testing could cause serious harm, including damage to the child's selfesteem and distortion of the family's perception of the child. This dominant view, however, has recently been criticised by, amongst others, Michie. She argues in favour of *empiricism* (Michie 1996: 178, 182). The dominant view, so she argues, implies that adults lose their right to have been tested in childhood. And with regard to the presumed harm to the child, she states: 'This may be true, but it may not be: We lack the evidence. There may also be benefits, such as giving more opportunity to prepare psychologically and practically for the future. Until we know what the actual, rather than the possible, effects are, we should avoid basing policy on speculation. (...) Caution in the absence of evidence is second best' (Michie 1996). Michie's view has been questioned by De Wert. He argues that even though it has not been *proven* that

presymptomatic testing in children for disorders like Huntington's disease harms the child, the risk that it does is substantial.
Evidence could only be obtained by an experiment with dispro-
portionate psychosocial risks for the child (De Wert 1999b).

Activity:

Suppose that parents ask you to test their little daughter for the
Huntington's disease mutation – would you perform the test or
not, taking into account the various pros and cons?

The view that the right of the child not to know should be
respected may have implications for prenatal diagnosis of
disorders with a later onset. After all, if a foetus is found to
carry the mutation for Huntington's disease, for example, and
the woman decides to carry the pregnancy to term, the right
of the child not to know will be violated.

Activity:

Please go back to the case of Patricia presented in the first chapter
(section 'Prenatal testing). Do you think that the dominant view,
that women should have access to prenatal diagnosis even if they
are not willing to consider termination of pregnancy, also applies
to the case of prenatal testing for Huntington's disease? Or is it
morally justified, in cases like this, to limit access to women who
intend to terminate pregnancy in the case of an unfavourable
result? Make a list of the arguments for and against, and explain
your view.

A different picture emerges with regard to predictive testing
for *childhood* disorders, especially if this allows for effective
preventive intervention. A good example is predictive testing
for multiple endocrine neoplasia 2A, an autosomal dominant
type of medullary thyroid carcinoma (see box below for some
background information).

Multiple endocrine neoplasia type 2A

Multiple endocrine neoplasia type 2A (MEN2A) is characterised
primarily by medullary thyroid carcinoma. The disease has an autosomal dominant pattern of inheritance. Consequently, children of

a carrier have a 50 percent chance of themselves being a carrier. The onset of the disease is highly variable: 50 percent of the carriers have a positive clinical test result for this carcinoma at the age of twelve, 80 percent at the age of twenty, and 95 percent at the age of thir-tyfive (Ledger et al. 1995). Since the discovery that MEN2A is caused by mutations in the RET proto-oncogene, carriers can be reliably identified by presymptomatic testing. Carriers can receive presymp-tomatic surgery. Life-threatening medullary thyroid carcinoma is no longer to be expected in those who have received this surgery.

Presymptomatic testing is considered to be clearly appropriate, as timely surgical intervention (thyroidectomy) substantially improves the prognosis for the 'carrier' child. In these kind of cases, the real question is not whether it is morally justified to test children at risk presymptomatically, but whether it is morally justified for parents *not to consent* to testing the child. In principle, parents do have the moral responsibility to consent to predictive testing that may clearly benefit the child at risk. If they refuse to give consent, the counsellor should point out the best interests of the child, and the parental responsibility to serve these interests. Appealing to the princi-ple of nondirectiveness would, in these cases, be mistaken.

A question needing further analysis is: what to do if the doctor's efforts to persuade the parents fail? Could a parental refusal to give consent for predictive testing ever constitute medical neglect? Would it be justified for the doctor to perform the test without parental consent? Some proponents of overruling parental autonomy in these cases refer to the case of Jehovah's Witnesses, whose refusal to consent to blood transfusion for their sick child need not be respected.

Activity:

Do you think that this is a valid analogy? Why (not)? Could over-ruling a parental refusal to give consent for predictive testing for a treatable childhood disorder ever be morally justified? If so, under which conditions?

Conflicting duties and responsibilities

As illustrated in the case below, presented by Louis Archer, in very rare situations a diagnostic test in a patient will reveal that a child (or the children) of the patient must carry the specific disorder as well. In other words, a diagnostic test for a parent may be an *'indirect' presymptomatic* test for the child.

The case of Thomas

A neurologist sent a blood sample to confirm a clinical diagnosis of Huntington's disease in a male patient, Thomas, aged forty-two years. His father and grandfather were also affected by Huntington's disease. Thomas already has two children, aged three and six years. The diagnostic test showed that Thomas was a 'homozygote' for the mutation, i.e., he had the mutation (the expanded CAG repeat) on both of the alleles. This was highly surprising, as this is very rare and no family history of Huntington's disease was found on the maternal side. The clinical geneticist was very worried about giving such a result to Thomas and his wife, as this would imply disclosing their children's genotypes. After all, the risk of any child of a homozygous individual being affected is virtually 100 percent. It is widely accepted that children should not be presymptomatically tested for adult onset disorders like Huntington's disease. In order to protect the children, however, the geneticist would have to withhold readily available information from the couple or even lie to them.

Activity:

Reflect on the following questions (put forward by Louis Archer) before reading the comment below: How would you counsel this couple? How would you solve the ethical dilemma between nonmaleficence (toward the children) and veracity (toward the couple)? Would you follow your prima facie duty as a medical geneticist and counsellor to fully inform the couple and explain to them the risks for their children? Or would you choose to protect the children from potential psychological damage at the cost of telling only half of the truth?

Heather Widdows gave the following commentary

This case brings up issues regarding the doctor/patient relationship and wider issues about the procedure and possible consequences of genetic testing.

The doctor-patient relationship (while paternalistic to differing extents in different European countries) is one that is grounded in trust. The patient expects to be told by the doctor all the relevant information pertaining to his/her condition. However, patients also expect doctors to act in their best interests, creating a conflict between the duty of care and the duty to tell the truth.

In this case, the 'homozygote' result was unexpected and therefore it is unlikely that the doctor discussed this possible outcome with the couple. (There is a secondary ethical issue here, whether a discussion should take place prior to testing to ascertain the extent to which the couple wish unsought information to be disclosed to them.) Assuming there was no prior discussion, the doctor has no information as to whether or nor the couple would like to be told such unexpected results, or whether they would wish to be left in ignorance (apart from the general impression s/he has about the couple and their beliefs; in practice it may be that this experiential and relational information is the most influential factor in the doctor's decision as to whether or not to tell the couple the full results).

Therefore, the doctor has to decide for him/herself which action is ethically correct. There are, broadly speaking, two possible choices:

Option 1: The doctor could simply inform the couple of the husband's condition, i.e., that the husband has tested positive for Huntington's disease. This would be giving the couple the test result, which they had agreed to receive, and would answer the question of whether the husband did/did not have Huntington's disease. After all, this provides the couple with the information they were seeking and it could be argued that providing any extra information is doing so without their consent and thus infringing upon their 'right not to know' and the child's right to an open future. In addition, the doctor may feel uneasy about giving the parents information about the children which the children do not have themselves. Accordingly, the doctor could argue that this very personal information should only be revealed to the affected children themselves and only when they reach maturity if they decide to be tested themselves.

Ethically these arguments are open to criticism. For example, many deny that the child does have an open future in a family that suffers from such a disease, because there is a constant awareness and fear of the disease. In addition, the right not to know is controversial. However, because this case is unusual it could be argued that the right not to know has more validity here. Unlike most situations, in this case the genetic information can be said to be predictive. Usually genetic information, while explanatory and useful with regard to outlining possibilities, does not provide certainty. However, in this case it does. Revealing the results discloses that the children's fate is determined.

A further reason the doctor may give for not fully informing the couple is that no treatment can be offered. Therefore, as there is nothing which the couple or the children can do to change their fate, providing them with such information can serve no purpose. It would only cause anxiety and anguish which would be against their best interests and so unethical.

Option 2: The doctor may feel that his/her duty is to give the couple all the information contained in the test results. S/he may feel to take any other option is effectively to lie to the couple. In opposition to the previous arguments, s/he may feel that the children do not have an open future anyway, given that they will already assume they have at least a 50 percent chance of developing Huntington's disease. Given this, the doctor may feel that giving the couple the information will not damage the children psychologically, but conversely that having the information at an early age will enable the children to adjust better to their situation. Having the information will enable them, as they grow up, to make life-changing decisions in ways which take into account their future life expectancy and quality. The doctor may also feel that the right not to know, while important, is in this case secondary to being able to make informed decisions.

The effect of changes

If the situation changes and the couple asks directly about the effects such results will have on their children, the doctor who initially chose 'option 1' may now wish to change his/her position. While willing not to disclose information that is not asked for, s/he may feel that not providing the information on request constitutes lying. If the doctor considers nondisclosure and lying to be ethically significantly distinct, then s/he may wish to change from option 1 and disclose fully.

(However, lying and non-disclosure are often held to be ethically the same, and doctors who initially opted for option 2 may regard any distinction as unethical.) Alternatively, the doctor may hold that not telling the couple is in their best interests and so act according to 'option 1', but when asked directly may consider not communicating the full information as a breach of trust. The doctor may consider protecting the bond of trust between the doctor and the couple to be more important than protecting the couple. However, the doctor may continue in accordance with 'option 1' if s/he bases her/his action on the conviction that this personal information should not be revealed to anyone other than the child, at a time when the child chooses to be tested.

If the couple express a wish to have more children, the doctor who had been happy to adopt 'option 1' in the first, or even the second, instance may change his/her position completely. In such a circumstance the doctor who had felt having the information was not in the couple's best interest may now change his/her position. In addition to concern for the couple, there is also concern for the future child. While nothing can be done to affect the fate of the two existing children, knowing this information could affect a future child, in that the couple might decide not to have more children or to use a form of assisted conception such as donor insemination. The impact the information may have on the couple's decision to have another child may convince doctors who would otherwise act according to 'option 1' to change their position.

Conclusion

There are strong ethical arguments for and against telling the couple the full results of the testing. Ethical factors which should be considered in this case are: truthfulness, trust within the doctor-patient relationship, the rights of the couple and the children to be given full information, and the rights of the couple and the children not to know. This case also brings up questions about the ramifications of genetic testing, especially the fact that genetic testing reveals unsought information not only concerning the individual who is tested but also other family members. Furthermore, in a wider context that case raises ethical questions, such as what duties individuals have to family and to society regarding sharing and acting upon genetic information. There are also philosophical questions, such as the relationship between genetic information and determinism, and the effects of a determined future on individuals.

There are some *controversial* exclusion criteria for presymptomatic testing for late onset disorders. One of these will be presented in the next case.

The case of Bob and Frank

In the first case in this chapter we met Bob, who has a 50 percent risk of carrying the Huntington's disease mutation. During the second counselling session, Bob told the doctor that he has a twin brother. The doctor asked Bob whether they were so-called 'monozygotic' twins, originating from one single embryo. The answer was affirmative. Clearly, the implication of this is that Bob and his brother have the same genetic status: if Bob proves to be a carrier, his brother will carry the mutation too. Bob informed the doctor that his brother does not want to be tested because he is afraid that he cannot handle an unfavourable test result. In view of this, the doctor became even more reluctant to perform the test.

Activity:

What is the central ethical issue here? Which ethical principles are at stake? How would you decide – and what are your main arguments? Reflect on these questions before reading the following.

Difficult conflicts can arise when presymptomatically testing the applicant will – or can – provide predictive information about the genetic status of another person at risk who has not requested the test, and who perhaps does not even want to know. Situations like these mostly involve applicants at 25 percent prior risk, whose parent at risk (50 percent) does not want to know his genetic status. A similar situation concerns a twin of a monozygotic twin pair at risk (50 percent) who applies for presymptomatic testing while the other twin does not want to know – like in the present case. Testing the applicant, i.e., respecting his right to know, may conflict with the relative's right not to know. Which (or whose) right should prevail? Fortunately, in many cases, counselling both parties involved results in a solution which is acceptable to all. In some cases, however, the conflict endures, and the counsellor has to make a difficult decision.

Ethical commentaries on this dilemma have, so far, focused mainly on Huntington's disease. On the one hand, it is argued that giving priority to the relative's right not to know is at odds with the principle of respect for the autonomy of the applicant. Furthermore, would it not constitute an intolerable breach of the principle of equal access to health care if persons presenting themselves for the test are selected according to whether or not their relatives claim the right not to know? On the other hand, proponents of a restrictive policy argue that the principle of nonmaleficence should take priority. Testing the applicant may cause the relative immense stress. In view of the complexity of these cases, a univocal guideline may not be appropriate.

Handling the current type of conflicts is especially difficult when the request concerns a late onset disease for which preventive or therapeutic measures are not (yet) available, like Huntington's disease. The availability of preventive measures, however, has moral relevance, in that the relative moral weight of the applicant's right to know will increase. As effective preventive methods emerge, e.g., for carriers of BRCA1/-2 mutations, overruling the applicant's right to know in view of a relative's right not to know will be increasingly difficult to justify.

II. Preparing for the test

Pre-test counselling
There is a strong consensus that predictive tests must be accompanied by appropriate genetic counselling. This principle has recently been adopted by the Convention on Human Rights and Biomedicine (Council of Europe 1996). The main purpose of pre-test counselling is to safeguard considerable deliberation and autonomous decision making. Counselling should include exploration of all pros and cons of testing. Furthermore, counselling should elucidate the motives of applicants for the test, helping the applicant to identify areas in which her/his expectations may be unrealistic.

Informed consent
The applicant's consent should be intentional, substantially free and based on substantial understanding. The pre-test

information to be provided to applicants for predictive BRCA1/-2 testing (as a condition for *valid* consent) has recently been presented by Geller et al (1997). Let us just tick off some of the relevant aspects. Firstly, applicants should realise that the predictive value of finding a pathological gene mutation is not established. Individuals with 'causal' mutations may have variable expression of the disease. In any case, recent studies suggest that the lifetime risks of mutation carriers are generally not as high as previously suggested (just over 50 percent for breast cancer, instead of 85 percent). Secondly, pre-test information should not focus exclusively on medical (genetic) aspects. Information about psychological, familial and social aspects is important too. It is especially important to inform applicants about possible socioeconomic consequences. Clinical experience has taught that many individuals at risk for a variety of inherited late onset disorders are not aware of the risk of insurance and employment discrimination, or tend to underestimate these issues (Chapter 4).

Time interval
In view of the complexity of the decision to submit to presymptomatic genetic diagnosis, informed consent may best be approached as a process. In general, it is desirable that there should be a substantial interval between the giving of the pre-test information and the decision whether or not to take the test.

The case of Elisabeth

Elisabeth is at 50 percent risk of the early onset variant of Alzheimer's disease (the box on p.31). Like Huntington's disease, this type of Alzheimer's disease is autosomal dominant, has a midlife onset, and is untreatable. When she applies for the presymptomatic test, the doctor informs her about the protocol. Elisabeth objects: 'But I want to be tested right now. I have been thinking about these issues for a long time, so I know what I am talking about!'

Activity:
Suppose you are the counsellor. Would you stick to the protocol/time interval or make an exception?

III. Informing about the results of the test

Respecting the right not to know

The individual tested has the right not to know, which includes the right to decide, on further consideration, that the result of the test shall *not* be given to him/her. Obviously, such change of mind will occur infrequently in case of adequate pre-test counselling.

Respecting confidentiality

Physicians occasionally feel the moral responsibility to convince the client to disclose relevant information to relatives who could benefit from that information or to grant permission for the physician to reveal this information. But what if the client refuses to do so? The issue of whether or not to inform relatives at high genetic risk against a client's wishes (or without his consent) is a difficult ethical dilemma because it poses a conflict between two well-known duties: the duty to preserve confidentiality and the responsibility to warn third parties of harm. The autonomy model may conflict with the view that, when dealing with genetic problems, at least to some extent the patient is *the family*.

Activity:

Before reading Kris Dierickx's overview, think about this ethical dilemma and try to formulate your own position.

In his paper, Kris Dierickx presented three different views regarding the question of whether a genetic counsellor should ever overrule the principle of respect for confidentiality of a client:

1) The first view holds that informational privacy/confidentiality is absolute, i.e., that it can never be overruled without the explicit permission of the individual. The foundation of this position lies in a specific concept of personal integrity, interpreted as the inviolability of a person's individuality.

2) Because of the nature of genes, it may, according to the second view, be argued that genetic information about any individual should not be regarded as personal, but as the common property of other people who may share those same genes, and who may need this information in order to find out their own genetic constitution. In this view the central

paradigm of genetic privacy is lineage and kinship. Genetic information is not a private possession, but a familial one. Accordingly, an individual has the moral duty to share information regarding his genetic constitution with others whose genetic make-up is similar. Of course, the moral duty to share genetic information with relatives does not entail a duty to share this information with other third parties (beyond one's family).

3) A third view holds that the principle of confidentiality is important, but not absolute. Internationally, there seems to be considerable support for the recommendation of the President's Commission that confidentiality can be overruled if (and only if) the following four conditions are met: a) reasonable efforts to elicit voluntary consent to disclosure have failed; b) there is a high probability both that harm will occur if the information is withheld and that the disclosed information will actually be used to avert harm; c) the harm that identifiable individuals would suffer if the information is not disclosed would be serious; d) appropriate precautions are taken to ensure that only the genetic information needed for diagnosis and/or treatment of the disease in question is disclosed (President's Commission 1983).

Obviously, handling concrete cases involves a delicate balancing of risks and harms.

Activity:

What do you think of these different views? Which view do you prefer? Let us assume that the third view is a reasonable 'middle of the road' position – how, then, should this view (in particular the President's Commission's recommendations) be applied in the context of genetic counselling for disorders like Huntington's disease, for which preventive and/or therapeutic measures are not available?

Guido de Wert presented the following commentary

The international guidelines for presymptomatic testing for Huntington's disease stress the priority of the principle of respect for confidentiality (International Huntington Association and World Federation of Neurology 1994). Some authors, however, consider breaching the duty to respect confidentiality to be justified, because it enables relatives to make an informed reproductive decision, thereby avoiding serious harm (Adams 1990). One may wonder, however, whether the invasion of confidentiality is justified in these cases. Firstly, apart from the harm to the next generation, there is nothing that can be done to avert harm to existing relatives. Unsolicited information can easily result in serious psychosocial problems, which is at odds with the professional duty of nonmaleficence. Secondly, one may well doubt whether breaching confidentiality would meet the condition that 'there is a high probability that … the disclosed information will actually be used to avert harm'. After all, experience with presymptomatic testing for Huntington's disease shows that at-risk persons regularly take the risk that they will transmit the mutation to the next generation.

Activity:

Confront your view with De Wert's argument. Would you now like to change your conclusions? If so, why? If you disagree, try to make your argument as strong as possible by questioning De Wert's arguments. Finally, apply the President's Commission's recommendations to the case of a woman who does not want her female relatives to be informed about their higher risk of carrying a BRCA mutation.

If the doctor holds the opinion that the principle of confidentiality can be overruled in some situations, this should be part of the informed consent process. Pre-test openness contributes to the client's well-informed decision making regarding submitting to the test, and may avoid future moral conflicts.

IV. Post-test counselling and evaluation

Any programme for predictive testing should be *integral* – i.e., it should encompass (the offering of) post-test counselling, as well as evaluation studies.

Post-test counselling

Post-test counselling serves various purposes. First, psychosocial counselling can help individuals to cope with the test result. This may be useful for carriers as well as *non*-carriers. A second purpose of post-test counselling concerns 'medical management'. After all, the major motivation for offering and applying for predictive testing is the hope that medical management, or adaptation of one's life style, following a 'positive' test result can prevent disease, or at least help reduce morbidity and mortality. The counsellor has the responsibility to provide clients with adequate and balanced information about the various options, and to help them to make a decision which best fits her (his) own values and preferences.

For women who carry a BRCA mutation, one of the options is a preventive ('prophylactic') mastectomy. This option has caused commotion in the media. Some commentators refuted this intervention in healthy women as 'bad medicine', on the grounds that it is mutilating and disfiguring and because its effectiveness is unproven. Others argue that this accusation is ill founded for various reasons. Firstly, even though the efficacy of this surgery still remains to be definitively established, there are, according to recent studies, strong indications that it does substantially reduce morbidity and mortality (Meijers-Heijboer et al. 2001). Secondly, one should respect the fact that carriers, in the face of a striking family history and close personal losses, may be unconvinced that screening (mammography, etc.) offers them the protection they desperately seek. Maybe it is not the (individual decision to opt for) surgery as such which needs ethical scrutiny, but the quality of the decision making process. While prophylactic surgery is an accepted part of the management of some cancer predisposition syndromes (e.g., multiple endocrine neoplasia 2A), discussion of these options should be highly individualised in hereditary breast/ovarian cancer (American Society of Clinical Oncology 1996).

Activity:

If you were a doctor confronted with a female carrier's request for preventive mastectomy, what would you do? Assuming that preventive surgery does offer more protection to carriers than regular medical exams, as a recent study suggests, would it be good medical practice to urge women to opt for surgery?

Evaluation studies

Discussion with carriers should emphasise the critical research needed to evaluate the pros and cons of predictive DNA testing and the efficacy of potential preventive measures in individuals at high risk. There are vital unanswered questions, both medical and psychosocial. What is the psychological impact of predictive testing (in females and males, in adults and in 'emancipated minors')? What is the predictive value of a 'positive' test? Which (genetic and nongenetic) factors determine the penetrance and the specific age of onset of the various mutations? How effective is prophylactic surgery? What is the preventive value of screening and/or modification of lifestyle (low-fat, high-fibre diets, regular exercise, etc.)?

In order to fully evaluate the presumed preventive value of certain modifications of lifestyle, it is important that individuals comply with and actually follow the recommended 'avoidance' strategy. Continuing support and regular reinforcement may be needed (Baird, 1990). Such reinforcement can take various forms, amongst others rational persuasion and manipulation. While rational persuasion is compatible with the principle of respect for autonomy, manipulation is not.

Activity:

At the beginning of this chapter, we asked you to sketch a protocol containing the main principles and guidelines for predictive genetic testing. Now that you have finished the reading of this chapter, we would like to ask you to go back to your protocol. Would you like to add, to amend, or to skip some guidelines? If so, make your reasoning explicit.

Both the first and the second chapter of this workbook concerned ethical issues in the field of *clinical* genetics, focusing on individuals requesting professional advice and, possibly, genetic testing. As we have seen, the individual cannot be isolated from his/her family, as genetic problems and information are by their very nature familial. In the next chapter, the focus will be broadened from the individual and his family to the level of the community. Interventions at this level belong to the field of *community* genetics.

Summary

In this chapter we dealt with:

- the different moral implications of presymptomatic testing for genetic disorders and of susceptibility testing.
- the debate on the inclusion and exclusion criteria for both kinds of testing (like competence, adulthood, etc.).
- the professional responsibilities of the counsellor before and after the genetic test.
- professional responsibilities regarding informing relatives at risk and the rule of confidentiality.

We have analysed these issues through several practical activities. We have discussed cases about predictive testing of adults for treatable and untreatable disorders, about the rights of children (not) to know their genetic status and the responsibilities of the parents, and about the conflict between the rule of confidentiality and the interest of family members in knowing their genetic status. Another activity was the making of a protocol for testing for predictive testing.

Suggestions for further reading

Chadwick R., Levitt M. and Shickle D. (eds) (1997). *The right to know and the right not to know.* Aldershot: Avebury.

Clarke A. (ed.) (1998). *The genetic testing of children.* Oxford, Washington DC: BIOS.

Kitcher P. (1996). *The lives to come: The genetic revolution and human possibilities.* New York: Simon & Schuster.

Marteau T., Richards M. (eds) (1996). *The troubled helix: Social and psychological implications of the new human genetics.* Cambridge: Cambridge University Press.

- 3 -

Population Screening and Genetic Community Research

In the previous chapters you have looked mainly at choices concerning individuals, but their families and communities were affected as well. In this chapter you will move on to topics in which the ideas of the patient's choice and autonomy are increasingly challenged. The perspective of a community makes explicit the fact that genetic information does not just involve individuals undergoing a screening, but is also relevant for families and communities as a whole. You will now focus primarily on populations and communities in which the need for careful balancing between individual and public interests is stronger.

In the first part of the chapter you will explore problems linked to genetic screening of a population – mostly special groups within a population – in order to detect particular diseases. In the second part of the chapter you will consider problems involved in genetic research with wide-ranging health-related aims.

Objectives

After reading this chapter you will be able to:

• understand the role and responsibilities of professionals in genetic population screening programs;

- evaluate the moral aspects of various genetic screening programs;
- assess the role of informed consent in genetic community research and 'gene banking';
- examine the moral issues of genetic community research in terms of risks and benefits;
- analyse the arguments 'pro' and 'con' the commercial use of genetic tests.

Population Screening

Genetic screening includes any kind of test performed for the systematic early detection or exclusion of a genetic disease, the predisposition or resistance to such a disease, or for determining whether a person carries a gene variant which may produce disease in his/her offspring. Screening may concern the general population or specific subpopulations defined on some basis other than their health. Genetic screening has to be differentiated from genetic testing because the implications are different. Genetic testing is carried out on patients who for whatever reason have taken the initiative and seek professional advice. With genetic screening people are asked to participate, and consequently tests may be seen to be imposed on individuals. Accordingly, the European Society of Human Genetics (ESHG 2000) has made a powerful argument for the fact that genetic screening has to be distinguished from genetic testing because the implications are different. The ethical dilemmas are magnified and the responsibilities for the physician correspondingly greater (The Nuffield Council 1993). The genetic nature of a disorder results in risk implications to family members of the person screened, even though they may not be, nor perhaps wish to be, included in the screening programme. Moreover, genetic screening does not necessarily lead to the prevention or treatment of diseases.

Screening for genetic conditions or genetic traits predictive of diseases is a medical act. As the public trusts the professional duty of care, a compliance effect may be expected when a screening test is offered, and this effect underlines the responsibility of professionals offering such tests.

A case from Finland[1]

In 1995 a screening programme for three genetic disorders – FraX (Fragile X Syndrome), AGU (Aspartylglycosaminuria), INCL (Infantile Neuronal Ceroid Lipofuscinosis) – was started in a town (population: 85,000) in Finland. Tests were offered to maternity clinic clients during the 8th–12th gestational week, among routine tests. Nurses informed the clients about the tests and disorders, and distributed leaflets describing the disorder, its risk, the test and finally the screening, which was said to be voluntary. The test was carried out during the next visit; 85 percent took the test, and screening went on smoothly for a year and a half.

The chief physician of the outpatients' clinic died, and the new physician began to question the screening practice. At this time the history of introducing and launching the screening was revealed. The screening programme had been initiated by a researcher/physician at the University Hospital. The physician had been active in the 1970s in launching Alpha-fetoprotein (AFP) screening. His colleague, the physician in charge of the outpatients' clinic, decided to start the AGU-screening. Two meetings with the maternity care staff took place before screening started. The screening had started before it was introduced to the local Board of Social Affairs and Health; and it was based on provisional authorisation by the Ethical Committee of the University Hospital. There were doubts among the nurses about the ethics of offering genetic screening as part of maternity care. The Board of Social Affairs and Health made a decision to discontinue the genetic screening programme after two years. Discontinuing the screening programme attracted publicity, and both the agents in initiating and running the screening and those criticising it (including critical mothers) could express their points of view.

Activity:

Consider the case and try to point out the most relevant issues emerging from it in the light of three different perspectives:

1) the roles of the professionals involved;

---

1   The case is based on the article 'Genetic screening in maternity care: preventive aims and voluntary choices', in press in *Sociology of Health and Illness*. It is used with the permission of the author, Piia Jallinoja (*piia.jallinoja@helsinki.fi*).

2) the goals of genetic screening;

3) the position of those it is being offered to, in this case a population of pregnant women seeking regular maternity care.

Now compare your remarks with the following ones:

1) The roles of the professionals involved:

The researcher/physician from University Hospital took advantage of the decentralisation of health care planning and organisation by launching a local screening programme. The decision to implement the screening in cooperation with a local chief physician and without informing the local authorities cannot be justified so easily. This course of action at least creates a conflict of duties for the members of the maternity care staff, especially for nurses. Is their – professional – autonomy being respected? Are they free to refuse participation in the project?

The nurses' positions with regard to the goals of genetic screening and the acceptability of certain screening methods should play an important role in the decision making process, as they are actually carrying out the screening and must take direct moral and professional responsibility vis-à-vis the clients/patients.

2) The goals of screening:

Prevention of disability and enhancement of the mother's choice are the goals mentioned in the programme. But an important aim failed to be considered: promotion of equity. A screening test should be offered to all those whose condition can be improved by making use of testing facilities. Though prima facie these goals may be regarded as beneficial, they need to be agreed by all those who are involved: researchers and institutions, nurses and physicians and patients.

3) The position of the pregnant women who are offered the screening:

In our case screening is being offered to pregnant women seeking regular maternity care. Are these women free to decide to take the test or to decline it? They come for routine care; 99 percent of pregnant women do so. These women are put under strong pressure and they are actually disempowered by the option offered, since they are not really free to make their own decision.

Reflect on how presenting screening as a 'routine' test is highly misleading. Here you see how in practice boundaries between genetic testing and genetic screening can become blurred. People are increasingly aware of tests available and may ask for them. If these tests are not part of a validated routine screening programme, professionals have to be careful to consider and explain the clinical utility of the test for the individual requesting to be tested.

Potential benefit and harm of genetic screening

The benefits of genetic screening include presymptomatic detection of diseases or susceptibility to diseases, enabling prevention, early diagnosis, care and treatment; the detection of a genetic predisposition to adverse effects of environmental factors facilitates avoidance of harm, and detection of carrier status enables reproductive or lifestyle decisions.

The possible detrimental effects of genetic screening include anxiety raised by information which cannot be used to make positive personal choices about therapies or preventive measures, or which is difficult to understand and interpret; undue pressure on individual choice; social stigmatisation of persons at increased genetic risk; social stigmatisation of persons who might decline an offer of genetic screening; disclosure of information about family members who have not consented to testing; misuse of the information and discrimination based on the test results after disclosure to third parties such as insurers and employers (as you will see in Chapter 4).

According to several studies and guidelines (Nuffield Council on Bioethics 1993, British Medical Association 1998, European Society of Human Genetics 2000) a genetic screening programme should be launched only after some major criteria have been met.

1. A screening programme should be considered only if there is general agreement on the benefits expected from it, both from the point of view of the professionals and from the point of view of the patients and the community. The goals and the target population must be well defined.

2. There needs to be an important health problem in terms of number of people affected or severity of the health problem.
3. The predictive power and level of accuracy of the particular test have to be assessed.
4. Even if benefits outweigh harm, the screening test should be offered as an option and individuals must remain free to refuse the test after appropriate information and counselling. Newborn screening can be justified and strongly recommended if early diagnosis and treatment clearly benefit the newborn.
5. If treatment or preventive measures exist, they should be offered equitably and with minimal delay.
6. As far as the implementation phase is concerned, it has been suggested that a genetic screening programme should always be preceded by a pilot project on a subpopulation with an appropriate evaluation of the positive and negative outcomes at all levels. These include: evaluation of the test, its acceptability and uptake rate; validity of the test results; use of the test results in decision-making processes; psychosocial consequences of the screening test and its clinical validity; utility of the screening process; staffing necessary to run the programme, total programme cost. The results of the pilot phase have to serve as a basis for a final decision on whether to proceed or not, involving the health care providers and representatives of the patients in the decision-making process.

Activity:

Make a list of the main genetic tests you know about (or you deal with) and in each case analyse the test from the perspective of population screening, by answering questions such as: Is the disease an important health problem? Is there a recognisable latent or early symptomatic stage? Is there an effective treatment for patients once the disease is recognised? Is there a suitable test that will identify the disease in its early stages? Is the test acceptable to the population?

Types of genetic screening

A widely agreed classification makes the distinction between genetic screening *before* birth and genetic screening *after* birth

(British Medical Association 1998, European Society of Human Genetics 2000).

Genetic screening *before* birth includes screening on foetal cells in maternal blood, maternal serum screening, ultrasound screening, screening on foetal cells obtained after amniocentesis or chorionic villus sampling (CVS) and preimplantation genetic diagnosis. The major reason for genetic screening before birth is to detect genetic disorders during early pregnancy. Information can be provided to enable couples to consider termination or continuation of the pregnancy while the early diagnosis would allow appropriate plans to be made for treatment and follow-up.

Genetic screening *after* birth includes neonatal screening, carrier screening at antenatal clinics, preconceptional carrier screening, cascade screening, school age screening and adults screening. Genetic screening after birth has two purposes. First, it can confirm that the person tested either has, or does not have, certain genetic characteristics with implications for his/her own future health. The second reason for an adult to be tested is to see if his/her children will be at risk.

Screening before birth

Prenatal screening, which is already widely implemented, focuses on the early detection of serious disorders. It attempts to identify foetuses at an increased risk of anomalies based on family history or advanced maternal age, or screening tests such as maternal serum testing (and ultrasound). Methods of prenatal diagnosis must be safe and effective. The standard method for diagnosis in the high-risk group is amniocentesis.

Screening on fetal cells in maternal blood

Fetal cells can be identified in the maternal circulation and techniques can be used to identify aneuploidies, including Klinefelter's syndrome, Down's syndrome and trisomy 13 and 18 (but there is a concern that foetal cells may persist in the maternal circulation from a previous pregnancy). Even though this kind of screening is not yet properly developed, it will be valuable in the future as a noninvasive method.

Maternal Serum Screening

Amniotic fluid alphafetoprotein (AFP) has been shown to be associated with open neural tube defect pregnancies; low maternal serum AFP is associated with Down's syndrome.

They were found to be markers of Down's syndrome. These two markers, together with AFP and maternal age formed the basis of the 'triple test'. Since the late 1980s, amniotic fluid alpha-fetoprotein (AFP), raised maternal serum human chorionic gonadotrophin (hCG), and low unconjugated oestriol (uE3) – the three biochemical markers normally referred to as 'triple test' – have been adopted to determine the probability (with 85–90 percent accuracy) of the presence of anencephaly or spina bifida or (with 60–65 percent accuracy) of the presence of foetal Down's syndrome (Stranc and Evans 1998).

Screening of foetal cells obtained by amniocentesis or CVS

Prenatal diagnosis for chromosomal disorders is now widely offered to high risk groups, either defined by maternal age or by using risk calculations based on serum marker screening test results or measurement of the nuchal-translucency, or a combination of the three. Most women at risk of carrying an affected foetus with a chromosomal disorder are offered an invasive prenatal diagnostic test. Those tests, amniocentesis and chorionic villus sampling (CVS), carry a risk of procedure-related foetal loss, but this is increasingly reduced.

Screening after birth

As you have read, screening after birth includes neonatal screening, preconceptional carrier screening, cascade screening, school-age screening and adults screening. There are several types of screening after birth.

Neonatal tests

This screening is considered relatively uncontroversial, both because it is aimed at providing an adequate therapy and because it can sometimes be highly effective. Some disease conditions, such as PKU (phenylketonuria) and congenite hypothyroidism, can be dramatically improved by an early diagnosis and treatment. In these situations the chance of success with therapy is so high that some guidelines on genetic tests envisage the possibility for physicians to take a directional approach in persuading parents to consent, since benefits to the child are so evident and harm can be so easily avoided.

Sickle cell disease screening and congenital adrenal hyperplasia have been added to neonatal screening as well. The inclusion of screening for conditions such as cystic fibrosis and Duchenne muscular dystrophy is already a fact, even though it is disputed. For example, some have questioned whether the neonatal detection of cystic fibrosis affects its clinical course (Motulsky 1997). But even if there is no effective treatment for this and other genetic diseases detectable at birth, such as Duchenne muscular dystrophy, neonatal screening has sometimes been recommended so that parents can receive genetic counselling about future pregnancies.

Cystic fibrosis (CF)

Cystic fibrosis (CF) is the most common lethal inherited metabolic disorder in whites. CF is characterised by severe respiratory problems and inadequate pancreatic function, caused by accumulation of sticky mucus. The rationale for neonatal screening for CF is that very early detection and treatment may improve clinical outcomes for children with CF. It has been suggested that more research should be done on the benefits of neonatal screening. More research on psychological and medical consequences for carrier detection in neonatal screening is needed and audit procedures to ensure that parents give informed consent to neonatal screening have to be performed (NIH Consensus Development Conference on Genetic Testing for Cystic Fibrosis 1997).

Duchenne muscular dystrophy (DMD)

Duchenne muscular dystrophy (DMD) is characterised by a rapidly progressive muscle weakness. The disease frequently occurs among all world populations. The age at which clinical symptoms of DMD are first noted is usually between two and five years, there is normally no remission, and the life expectancy is approximately twenty years. Treatment is palliative, and it aims at managing the symptoms. Even if testing at birth is controversial, since there is no advantage for newborns, neonatal screening allows parents to receive genetic counselling about future pregnancies.

Fragile X syndrome

Fragile X syndrome is the most common cause of mental retardation from a single gene defect. The major features are learning disability of varying severity, behavioural problems such as hyperactivity and autistic tendencies, and physical characteristics. Although Fragile X syndrome is not curable there are a number of medical, educational, psychological and social interventions that can improve the symptoms.

Screening for Fragile X is more widely accepted as an antenatal test for detecting female carriers. Conversely, neonatal and paediatric screening of high-risk groups raise questions on the justification of diagnostic testing in individuals who are suspected of having the syndrome. As there is no cure, there may be little value in accurate diagnosis. The debate against screening has been centered around the potential stigmatisation of Fragile X syndrome patients.

School age and adult screening

For adolescents and adults there is a possibility of presymptomatic detection of late-onset diseases such as familial hypercholesterolaemia and hemochromatosis. Screening for late-onset diseases at birth, although increasingly possible, has never been recommended, because preventive treatments often do not exist or, if available, are best carried out later in life. Genetic counselling of parents regarding the risk of a disease in a child that manifests itself many decades later is rarely requested or considered (Motulsky 1997). Screening for late-onset diseases raises complex ethical issues with regard to informed consent, privacy of genetic information and confidentiality of test results.

Familial hypercholesterolaemia (FH)

Familial hypercholesterolaemia is an autosomal dominant disorder characterised by elevation of serum cholesterol bound to low-density lipoprotein (LDL). Genetic screening for familial hypercholesterolaemia may be appropriate since risk of early coronary artery disease (CAD) is considerably increased by the mutation of a single gene.

Population-based genetic screening for FH is not practical because of the large number of mutations causing this disorder. However, in some populations most cases of FH can be explained by only one or a few mutations. Examples include the Finns, the French Canadians and the Christian Lebanese. In these populations the frequency of FH is higher than that generally accepted in western countries.

Hemochromatosis

Hemochromatosis is a disorder of iron metabolism that increases iron absorption and results in excessive iron accumulation. Clinical manifestations range from lethargy and abdominal pain to arthropathy, diabetes, hypogonadism, skin pigmentation, cardiomyopathy, and hepatic fibrosis and cirrhosis. Some guidelines consider that population-based genetic screening for hemochromatosis is not justified at present, due to uncertainties about gene mutations and the optimal care of asymptomatic people. Moreover, genetic screening raises concerns regarding possible stigmatisation and discrimination.

Predispositional tests

Predispositional screening measures the higher or lower probability for an individual to be susceptible to a pathology derived from a complex, multifactorial etiology, such as heart disease, which partially depends on a genetic predisposition as well as on behaviour, diet and the environment. In this case the weight of the genetic factor is very difficult to be evaluated, since the mere fact that the individual is more likely to develop heart disease does not mean that he/she will develop such a disease. So, given the lack of predictive quality and reliability of this information, one should be careful not to label an individual as 'at risk' in an arbitrary way.

Cancer susceptibility

Cancer susceptibility may be seen in different ways if considered from the point of view of individual testing than if considered from a population screening point of view. Some people may inherit abnormal genes, which predispose those individuals to a high risk of certain malignancies: the hereditary cancers include (but are not limited to) ovary, breast, colon, endometrium and, to a lesser extent, prostate, skin and pancreas.

However, population screening for cancer susceptibility remains controversial. The benefits and limits of testing, and the range of prevention and treatment are different in each hereditary tumour. Further research is needed to continue the analysis of the significance (frequency or penetrance) of mutations of cancer predisposition genes and to clarify the genotype-phenotype and other correlations.

Carrier screening

Carrier screening programmes attempt to detect individuals who carry a disease-related allele in order to inform them about their specific risk and help them make reproductive choices accordingly. Carriers are phenotypically normal and show no signs of the disease, but such individuals would be at risk of having children with the disorder.

If carrier screening is initiated during pregnancy and the result is abnormal, a test on the male partner follows. If both partners are carriers, they are informed of the possibility of a test on the foetus.

But screening can be done before pregnancy in order to allow a wide choice of reproductive options. Some autosomal recessive diseases are often restricted to certain ethnic or racial groups, such as the thalassaemias, sickle cell anaemia and Tay-Sachs disease. Population screening for heterozygous carriers is aimed at identifying carriers who are at risk of having an affected child if the other parent is also a carrier. In communities where the risk of serious genetic disorder is high, preconceptional carrier screening may be desirable.

Some carrier screening programmes – such as thalassaemia – have largely taken place in some countries, sometimes in schools. This approach turned out to be highly effective for the disorder to become less common. However, this practice has also revealed the potentiality for discriminatory actions when focused on special groups (such as African-Americans in the United States during the 1970s).

It can also be argued that introducing screening tests in schools, i.e., on very young people, should not be done until the minor may give a fully understood and informed consent. Moreover, the psychological effects of getting knowledge about carrier status are relevant, either in terms of anxiety or of better adaptation; therefore screening must always be accompanied by adequate counselling and public education.

Activity:

1. Consider the most relevant features of different types of screening and try to assess the pros and cons of launching a screening programme for each case.

2. Make a comparison of different situations in which antenatal, neonatal or preconception tests should be performed. Consider the variety of reasons for acting carefully when introducing predisposition screening.

3. Susceptibility and predisposition screening raise concerns about transforming everyone in the population into a patient. Does genetic screening medicalise society at large?

Genetic Community Research

Beginning with the Human Genome Project (HUGO), researchers have focused on genetics not only for specific medical purposes, but in order to acquire wider knowledge on the genetic structure of different human populations. For instance, the Human Genetic Diversity Project (HGDP) was aimed at determining the variability within the human genome of different, and specially isolated, populations.

As an introduction to population genetics, we are asking you now to read the following paper by Ruth Chadwick. Chadwick's arguments will provide fertile grounds for discussing some of the main issues involved in the increase of programmes aimed at large-scale evaluation of the genetic diseases that may possibly affect a population or, by and large, its genetic make-up.

Paper for discussion

Genetic databases

R. *Chadwick*

*(Institute for Environment, Philosophy and Public Policy,
Lancaster University, UK)*

What is meant by the terms 'genetic databases', 'DNA banking' and 'gene banking' is not always clear. What is clear however, is that there are two sets of issues – those concerned with the setting up of sample collections, and those that are information collections. There is overlap between these sets of issues, but they are not identical.

Where information databases are concerned, it is arguable that current research in the biological sciences is leading to a new scientific paradigm. Whereas traditionally research was conducted by the testing of hypotheses in the laboratory, followed by the publication of results in peer reviewed journals, the establishment of large databases is facilitating their use to both generate and test hypotheses. In the context of the new science the question arises as to how the principles of the conduct of traditional science and the paper record can be transferred to and maintained.[2]

In parallel, however, there are developments that are producing new paradigms in ethics. This is not surprising, because developments in science and technology have a 'value impact' – they can change the way we look at things and call for new principles to mediate between the competing interests at stake, for a key task of ethics is to mediate between interests. Ethics has both to identify the interests and find principles to mediate between them.

In the developments under way in the biological sciences, the interests at stake include those of research participants (individuals and groups); the interests of academic science; the interests of commercial organisations; and the interests of the community in, for example, public health.

The collections with which I shall be primarily concerned in this paper relate to collections of DNA samples, but some

---

2   I owe this point to a contributor at the Bordeaux Colloquium preceding the meeting of the Ministers of Research of the G8 countries, June 2000.

of the most complex ethical issues arise when these are linked with health records. It has become clear that the principles of biomedical ethics which have been highly regarded for some time, such as that of individual informed consent, may not be ideally equipped to deal with issues that arise in large-scale population genetic research. Indeed, in the course of collecting samples for such research it is frequently necessary to seek the consent of a community rather than of individuals, and this inevitably gives rise to issues of definition of both 'community' and 'consent'.[3]

In this context there is a self-conscious search on the part of some bodies for a more relational approach to ethics that takes into account concepts and values such as what benefits the community can and should expect in the context of a situation in which the benefits (and risks) of participating in research projects may be of a significantly different kind than the traditional model.

Database initiatives

There has been considerable debate about proposals to set up health care databases in different countries, the one that has given rise to the most controversy being in Iceland.[4] In that country the Parliament passed in 1998 the Health Sector Database Act, by which the Health Minister was given the authority to grant an exclusive licence to a for-profit corporation to set up and maintain a database of the health records of all Icelanders.

In the United Kingdom, proposals have been made by the Medical Research Council (MRC) and the Wellcome Trust for a national database involving a collection of DNA samples which will be linked with National Health Service records (Farrar 1999). This, it is proposed, would be run by a public-private consortium. Database initiatives have also been proposed elsewhere, e.g., Sweden and Estonia (Annas 2000). There already exists one population gene bank in the United Kingdom, in the form of the North Cumbria Community Genetics Project (North Cumbria Community Genetics Project 2000). This is a joint project between the Genetics

---

3   See the discussion in the HUGO Ethics Committee Statement on Benefit Sharing (2000).

4   See the websites of Mannvernd and deCode.

Unit at the Westlakes Research Institute and the Departments of Genetics and of Child Health at the University of Newcastle.

Similarities and differences between initiatives

Arguably different cultural contexts raise different issues in the regulation of the creation of genetic databases. It has been suggested, for example, that the longstanding interest in genealogy that exists in Iceland makes it more likely that the population will be welcoming the health sector database. Claims have also been made about Icelanders' lack of interest in privacy issues. It has also been suggested that the relative isolation of the Iceland population makes it particularly likely to generate useful results, though this is contested (Specter 1999).

Apart from the contextual factors there are differences in the ways in which it is proposed the databases will be run. One such issue concerns public-private involvement. One of the points of controversy concerning the Iceland initiative has been the strong position of a single company, namely deCode. The United Kingdom proposals emanating from Wellcome and the MRC seek to avoid this.

Other issues concern the regulatory requirements and the mechanisms for collection of samples (informed consent or not?) and for protecting confidentiality and/or privacy. In the North Cumbria Community Genetics Project, samples are being collected from the afterbirths of thousands of newborns, together with blood samples from the mothers, with their consent. Confidentiality is protected in the following way: each pregnancy is identified by a project number only, which links the mother's data with her baby's samples. The data and samples are held separately.

Activity:

In the section 'Suggestions for further reading' at the end of this chapter you will find a series of national or international documents, which establish guidelines on the topics here explored. Read a couple of them and make a comparison between the different adopted positions on the issue of protection of confidentiality.

The Wellcome Trust/MRC initiative proposes to collect samples with informed consent. In Iceland it has been a matter of controversy that entry into the health sector database was to be by presumed consent, although actual DNA samples would be collected using informed consent and there has been some confusion about this in the discussion. It has been argued by deCode that, in epidemiological study using health records, to demand informed consent is not and never has been the norm.

Activity:

Reflect on the differences that Chadwick is pointing out:

1. The creation of a number of biobanks – term which refers to all collections of human biological materials (HBMs) – raises a variety of ethical and legal concerns, particularly where individual and (in many cases) group consent, reliability of anonymisation procedures, and legitimacy of secondary uses are concerned. Make a comparison with what has been written in the book on 'Ethics of Research'.

2. Discuss the North Cumbria Community and analyse the differences with the deCode case.

Now continue with Chadwick's text and read her reflections.

The issues

The desirability and value of databases is hotly contested. They give rise to debate about both the potential harms and benefits.

Concerns

The concerns that have been put forward relating to genetic databases have for the most part focused on the potential harm to the individual (Chadwick 1999). Because it is known that there are risks arising out of access to genetic information, both by the individual subject and by third parties, much attention has been paid to confidentiality and privacy issues. Although these two concepts are not the same, they have not always been clearly distinguished in the debate. Also, because the databases are going to be used for research purposes, the individuals who donate samples are research subjects. This gives rise to issues about research ethics, with particular reference to informed consent.

In addition to the potential harms to individuals, however, there are worries about the implications for groups and communities. Results of genetic research could characterise whole groups, e.g., Icelanders, in ways that might not be advantageous to them (Annas 2000). Where for-profit companies stand to gain considerable commercial advantage, there have been concerns that groups or communities are being 'commodified' or 'exploited' without adequate warrants.

Potential harms have also been identified in relation to particular social institutions or practices. The Iceland health sector database has been criticised for its potential impact on scientific freedom. The practice of science as an institution depends on freedom of access to samples and information for research. The extent to which scientific freedom is at risk is, however, hotly contested.[5]

The practice of health care, also, is arguably under threat. In Iceland the doctor–patient relationship might be affected by the establishment of the Health Sector Database. As already suggested, principles of medical ethics, e.g., confidentiality and informed consent, might need adjustment in the light of changing circumstances and the spin-offs for the ethics of medical practice more generally are difficult to predict.

Benefits

On the other hand there are suggestions that genetic databases are the basis of 'smart' health care in the future (Fears and Poste 1999). By linking genetic information with health care records and patterns of disease, it is hoped to establish what are the genetic bases of common diseases, including cancer and heart disease. Beyond that, it is argued that information about the genetic basis of drug response should open the way to more effective and safer prescribing, and the genetically informed development of therapeutic products.

There is a question, however, about who the interested parties are to whom these benefits are likely to accrue. There are clearly considerable commercial interests at stake, and in

---

5 See footnote 3.

the Iceland case the potential profit of the single company involved has been one of the points of contention. It is argued by that company that Icelanders as a whole also stand to benefit, including advantages in the form of free drugs for Icelanders, provision of jobs and better health care. Arguably, also scientific progress is served by such initiatives, in the light of what has been said above about changing scientific paradigms.

Perspectives on the issues

The question arises as to how we call and should assess these concerns and benefits. It is fair to say, I think, that up to now the predominant approach to the issues in the literature has been what I call a 'harm-centred approach' – what are, for example, the potential harms to individuals, in the form of risks to their privacy and autonomy, and how can we introduce safeguards. This is, perhaps increasingly, challenged by a 'benefit-sharing' model, which not only argues that there are potential benefits from these developments but also looks at how they are and should be distributed.

Thus the HUGO Ethics Committee, for example, issued a statement in April 2000 on benefitsharing, recognising concerns that have been voiced around the world – in particular concerning groups and communities whose samples might be incorporated into databases, leading to discoveries which are likely to make large profits for commercial organisations. The Ethics Committee argued that there is a case for such companies to make some return to communities that have contributed samples. The same considerations apply to individuals, but the Committee acknowledged the practical and moral difficulties in either compensating or rewarding particular individuals. Practical problems include the problem of identification of individuals – for one thing, useful discoveries may not be made for long periods of time. In any case, depending on how samples are stored and used, identification of individuals may not be feasible. From a moral point of view, the individuals whose samples form the basis of a major discovery may have contributed no more, in terms of effort, than those whose samples do not. There are issues here about what the basis of reward or compensation should be. The HUGO Ethics Committee therefore, as one of its recommendations, suggested that companies should consider donating between 1 and 3 percent of their net profit to humanitarian causes.

One potential problem with the turn to a benefit-sharing model is that the concerns about potential harms do not simply disappear – so what is the relation between the two? Annas, in his discussion of what principles might be appropriate in this area, suggests that '...research should not be conducted on a population, even research related to migration patterns or the evolution of a genome, unless the benefit to the population is likely to outweigh the risks' (Annas 2000). If it is to be thought of in terms of a trade-off, however, the possibility clearly exists that the emphasis on distribution of benefits will be seen not as an exercise in distributive justice, but as an attempt to buy people off. The harms therefore need to be explicitly addressed.

There have of course been attempts to look at how informed consent and confidentiality might be adapted to the new setting, e.g., by the Medical Research Council in the United Kingdom (MRC 1999), and by the National Bioethics Advisory Commission in the United States (NBAC 1999). What are the issues specific to databases that require such adaptation?

It has already been mentioned that community consent has come under discussion as a possibility (Weijer 1999). Annas takes the view that while a community may approve, it may not legally consent and so the issue remains one for individual consent. There are specific issues to consider. One is the extent to which individual subjects whose samples are to be stored should have information about the type of research that might be done on their samples. This affects, for instance, the extent to which it is possible to opt out of particular studies, with which they might not be in sympathy – for example, suppose someone supports research on the genetic basis of heart disease, but not on genetic factors involved in alcoholism. Alternatively, they might want to withdraw from the database as a whole. Another issue concerns the extent to which individuals should have access to feedback about what has been discovered about their individual samples and what information is to be given about this. The possibility of feedback, however, is clearly in tension with the possibility of anonymity, which is a safeguard against the potential harm arising out of misuse of genetic information. A third issue concerns the incorporation of samples in databases from those who are unable to give a valid consent. The North Cumbria Community Genetics Project (2000) takes the following approach:

'Consent is given for the collection and storage of samples and personal information for use in genetic and epidemiological research studies approved by the West Cumbria Local Ethics Research Committee. Individuals opt into the project as a whole but cannot opt out of specific studies. However, if a mother wishes to withdraw from the whole project she can do so at any time. The mother's consent is on behalf of the child and the consent form clearly states that research using the samples collected may involve reference to the health records of herself and her baby'.

There are also, however, reasons for thinking informed consent is particularly problematic in this context more generally: the degree of public awareness of genetics; the sensitivity of the 'information'; doubts about whether it is *possible* to be informed in this field.

Public awareness and understanding of genetics

There are different aspects to the debate about public understanding. The first relates to worries that genetics is not only poorly understood but that it is also difficult to understand. Despite the claim of the gene's role as a cultural icon (Nelkin and Lindee 1995), the explanation of what a gene is is no simple matter. Thus individuals may have a very imprecise idea of what they are consenting to regarding genetic information. One possible construct of the situation is that people are being sold a narrative of progress in connection with the Human Genome Project, portrayed as the answer to disease (via the promises of gene therapy and designer drugs). On the other hand there is concern, e.g., in the United Kingdom, that individuals have lost trust in science and therefore in the genetic 'information' they are given.

An important distinction must be drawn, however, between the information required for a better understanding of genetics per se and the information necessary for individuals to appreciate the implications of genetic information for themselves.

The nature of the information

The second concern about consent in relation to genetic research is that genetic information is particularly sensitive. The considerations that support the (not uncontroversial) view that genetic information is different from other medical information have included the facts that we share genetic information with relatives and that it is not specific to time. This gives such information a predictive aspect, for both individual patients and their relatives, which in turn makes the dangers arising out of disclosure particularly acute because of the possibility of adversely affecting the future course of someone's life.

Some have argued for a right not to know such information (Chadwick et al. 1997). While all these features may to a greater or lesser degree be true of other medical information, what does seem to be the case is that these features give rise to different possible interpretations and implications, which may make more likely the unintentional inflicting of harm by researchers.

Another worrying feature of genetic information is the potential way in which it is perceived as intricately bound up with our identities as persons. It has been suggested that DNA is the modern secular equivalent of the soul, or at any rate the guarantor in some sense of who we are (cf. Nelkin and Lindee 1995). However well grounded this view may or may not be, in this respect the information takes on new significance which may affect the nature of informed consent. This suggests the need at least for special care in informing research participants about what will become of their samples.

Is it possible for anyone to be informed?

The third concern about the possibility of being 'informed' in this area relates to the idea that it is simply not possible to be genuinely informed of all the risks and benefits in genetic research. The idea behind this concern is that no one can be adequately informed, because it is not possible to foresee the range of uses to which genetic information about someone might be put. It is necessary here to address specifically an important difference between 'narrow' consent related to a specific condition and 'broad' consent on an unspecified range of conditions. It might be argued that it is only broad consent to which this worry relates. On the other hand, even in the case of narrow consent to genetic research on a specific condition, individuals are making choices about their samples in an uncertain situation. It is nevertheless possible to inform research participants of the type of research, its risks and benefits, and implications for them. It is at this point that we need to turn to a specification of the nature of those risks and benefits.

Activity:

Stop again for a moment and discuss the issue of informed consent to genetic community screening. There are a number of questions to be addressed:

1. Should consent be asked from every single individual involved in the project? Is this not too complicated when a large population is involved?

2. Can we substitute individual consent by *community consent*?

3. What reasons can be given for separately addressing individual and group consent?

4. How can group consent be defined and on which conditions can it be considered valid?

Is the notion of self-determination relevant for communities and groups, similar to the concept of autonomy for individuals?

Chadwick's paper proceeds by examining the risks and benefits involved in genetic community screening:

The nature of the risks and benefits

It might be helpful to begin by examining a list of concerns typically expressed about genetic research. The list of concerns found in the HUGO Statement on the Principled Conduct of Genetic Research provides a fairly typical list of the kind of potential harms arising from genetic research (HUGO 1996):

● Fear that genome research could lead to discrimination against and stigmatisation of individuals and populations and be misused to promote racism

- Loss of access to discoveries for research purposes, especially through patenting and commercialisation
- Reduction of human beings to their DNA sequences and attribution of social and other human problems to genetic causes
- Lack of respect for the values, traditions and integrity of populations, families and individuals
- Inadequate engagement of the scientific community with the public in the planning and conduct of genetic research

While some of these may be several stages removed from a given individual asked to consent to provide a sample for genetic research, it is arguably because of these wider implications that the issue of informed consent is thought to be particularly problematic in the genetic context. Discrimination, in particular, is a live issue relevant to the consent process. It is to a large extent because of the potential for stigmatisation and discrimination, e.g., from insurers and employers, that the informed consent issues involved in genetic research have been so concerned with privacy and confidentiality. The question of racism is also an important one in so far as individuals who have not consented to participate in particular research projects may be affected by it, because, for example, a research project may result in information showing that there are predispositions to particular conditions or treatments that are specific to certain minority ethnic groups. This information may be disadvantageous (as well as having potential advantages to people seeking information facilitating their own health-related decisions) not to individuals participating in the trial but to members of the group generally.

An alternative approach

While one option is to look at how informed consent can be managed in the light of these complicating factors, an alternative is to look at whether existing principles of medical ethics can cope. Some bodies are self-consciously looking for alternative principles, such as the following:

- Solidarity – state protection against genetic discrimination in exchange for participation of citizens

- Equity – universal access and availability of genetic tests and treatment and societal sharing of the benefits of research[6]

Others have suggested that instead of increasing the amount of information given in the attempt to achieve informed consent, and in the light of the search for mechanisms to protect confidentiality, what is needed is a re-examination of what it means to respect persons in the context of the establishment of large-scale genetic databases.[7]

Conclusion

There seem therefore to be a number of options:
- Retain the harm-centred approach to the issues and examine what safeguards are needed in the light of the complexity of the issues surrounding genetic databases
- Introduce an explicit focus on benefit sharing and address the relationship between benefits and potential harms
- Conduct an analysis of the extent to which it is true that there is a new scientific paradigm emerging which might in turn suggest that traditional principles might need to be rethought in the context of genetic databases.

Chadwick's paper provides a number of interesting questions to discuss. The following two sections focus on two particular topics. The former deals with problems of race and discrimination; the latter refers to some problems involved in commercial exploitation of genetic screening and information.

Genetic Research and Ethnicity

An aspect of genetic community research deals with genetic diversity among different ethnic groups. This situation is more likely to happen in international research, and consequently it does not seem to affect everyday physicians' work. However, in contemporary multicultural society, genetic community research is likely to target a population in a national context and to happen through GPs' activities.

---

6 Bartha Knoppers at the Bordeaux Colloquium.
7 Onora O'Neill, presentation at the American Society of Bioethics and Humanities.

The National Bioethics Advisory Commission (NBAC), in its document on Ethical and Policy Issues in International Research (2000), has pointed out general criteria both for assessing the acceptability of a research programme and for adequately approaching the population to be involved. In order to be approved, a research programme needs to be scientifically sound even in its social impact and consequences, namely it has to present a favourable risk-benefit ratio, it must provide a fair distribution of benefits and burdens, and it must be widely explained and disclosed to the population before informed consent is sought. This means that researchers have to approach the group or the population they wish to collaborate with well before the beginning of the research. First of all researchers have to address the community as such – through its representatives, where they can be legitimately recognised – and look for a general, collective consent. This step should be taken well in advance, so that a public discussion may happen and the community may become aware of the content and purpose of the proposed project. Individual informed consent, that is always considered as a necessary step and that cannot be subsidised by collective agreement, should be obtained shortly before or at the time of sampling (see also Morrison Institute 1997).

The increasing concern for the respect that indigenous and traditional cultures deserve made scientists more aware that the relevance of genetic research should not be taken for granted and that it represents the Western cultural point of view on knowledge. Moreover, researchers should be alerted on the potentiality for discrimination involved in defining groups or special populations.

The Commercialisation of Genetic Screening

Medical interest, patients' demand, or awareness of the available testing opportunities are factors which may lead to an increase in the genetic tests market. However, given the amount of financial investment in the area, many fear that a myriad of novel genetic services will be offered to the public before the legal and social ramifications have been fully explored. Marketing and advertising strategies used by the biotech/pharmaceutical industry are also criticised as an inappropriate means of conveying medical information. Patients can be mostly perceived as 'clients' or 'consumers'.

Moreover, concern exists also for issues of ownership or, broadly speaking, of control on genetic information. Indeed, after the European Directive on the patentability of biotechnological inventions has been enacted in 1998 (Directive 98/44/EC), genetic sequences are considered as patentable matters. Even though individuals are not entitled to get financial benefits from their own biological materials (Council of Europe 1996), a widely accepted position states that disclosure of economic interests should be considered an essential feature of informed consent. Individuals have to be informed about the potential economic exploitation of genetic information and to give their consent. Where consent is presumed this requirement cannot be properly met.

Patents on genes are highly contested for the unique market position which patents may grant. Moreover, they seem to create a tension between physicians and patients. However, something has been changing in this conflict recently.

The Case of Pseudo Xanthoma Elasticum (PXE)

Patrick Terry considers himself as a father and a lay person (not an expert), as the PXE International administrator, as a research participant and researcher, as a consultant to private and public entities, and as the founder of a start-up biotechnology company. Terry and his wife have taken on these additional roles because their children suffer from Pseudo Xanthoma Elasticum (PXE), a genetic disorder affecting skin and eyesight and eventually leading to blindness. To fight PXE, the Terrys built an international Internet movement in order to find a therapy for the disease.

Their efforts paid off big in October 1999, when a University of Hawaii researcher, who received samples from Terry's group, discovered the PXE gene. But what grabbed the attention of the world of genetics – as well as those in the intellectual property realm – was the news that Sharon Terry and the researcher had filed a joint application to patent the gene.

> Terry had set up the blood and tissue bank so that every scientist who used its samples would be required to share any intellectual property claims with the organisation, to which Terry assigned the patent rights.

The 'PXE Model' is being used to inform other groups in the Genetics Alliance (http://www.geneticalliance.org), a network of 300 groups organised around rare genetic disorders. They are being approached by indigenous groups in order to generate ideas on how to make research a community endeavour (Solovitch 2001).

The partnership realised between patients and researchers in the PXE case is considered to be an attempt to overcome unfairness in genetic property and to share both scientific and economic benefits from genetic advancement. It also allows people suffering from genetic diseases (especially rare diseases) to be more actively involved or even to be a driving force in research.

However, the case raises some doubt as well, insofar as it may provoke other forms of genetic exploitation or the implicit selling of human biological materials.

Activity:

1. Do you think that 'genetic consumerism' is an actual risk?

2. What do you think of the benefit sharing realised in the PXE case? Is this coalition between patients and physicians ethically acceptable and on which conditions?

Summary

In this chapter we have dealt with:

- two main issues where the communitarian dimension – and possibly its clashing with individual autonomy – emerges as a special feature of genetics, namely population screening and genetic community research;

- the special attention that population screening requires, as far as a higher degree of scientific uncertainty is involved, a different balance between costs and benefits exists both

for individuals and their communities, and few or (sometimes) no therapies are available;
- the fairly recent developments of genetic community research, where the main goal is to improve knowledge in the genetic field and about genetic diversity;
- the economic implications of genetics, with the risk involved in "genetic consumerism", but also with the substantial benefits stemming from a more equitable relation between science and society.

We have presented and discussed the ethical implications of population screening and genetic community research with the main aim of showing how individual autonomy requires to be outweighed with communitarian values. Accordingly, these two issues need to be analysed not only as moral problems, but as policy-relevant subjects as well (and they are widely treated by legal documents). Moreover, we have outlined that scientific uncertainty is higher in dealing with the generality of genetic data, and due ethical concern has to be given to this lack of reliable knowledge. A third caveat is linked to market implications of genetics.

Despite all these troublesome concerns, we exposed some arguments and cases about ways for individual and collective ends to fairly meet.

Suggestions for further reading

Main documents on bio-banks and the protection of privacy

United States

Department of Health and Human Services, Office of the Secretary (2000). 45 CFR Parts 160 and 164 Standards for Privacy of Individually Identifiable Health Information. *Federal Register*, **65**(250) December 28, 82462.

European Union

Directive 95/46/EC of the European Parliament and of the Council of 24 October 1995 on the protection of individuals with regard to the processing of personal data and on the free movement of such data.

Opinion of the European Group on Ethics in Science and New Technologies to the European Commission (1998). *Ethical Aspects of Human Tissue Banking.*

Council of Europe

Recommendation No. R (97) 5 and Explanatory Memorandum of the Committee of Ministers to Member States on the Protection of Medical Data (13 February 1997).

Canada

Tri-council Policy Statement (Medical Research Council of Canada, Natural Sciences and Engineering Research Council of Canada, Social Sciences and Humanities Research Council of Canada) (August 1998). *Ethical Conduct for Research Involving Humans.*

Iceland

Act on Biobanks no.110/2000.

Hugo Ethics Committee Statement on DNA Sampling (February 1998). *Control and Access.*

Khourry M.J., Burke W. and Thomson E.J. (eds) (2000). *Genetics and Public Health in the 21st Century.* New York: Oxford University Press.

– 4 –

The Social Use of Genetic Information

Thus far we have dealt with the search for genetic determinants of specific diseases in the context of health care. We have presented the ethical issues of genetic diagnosis and screening as instruments to predict the probability of certain diseases in order to help the client to make informed decisions about his or her own health care, health behaviour or his or her reproductive decisions. However, the use of genetic information is not limited to the context of health care and reproduction. There is an important area in our society where genetic information is used for other purposes, namely the access to social goods. The most important areas where the social use of genetic information has become prominent are insurances and the selection of employees.

Objectives

After reading this chapter you will be able to:

- understand the moral issues of supplying information on the genetic status of applicants to insurance companies;
- analyse the arguments 'pro' and 'con' the use of force regarding the supply of genetic information to insurance companies;
- evaluate the moral implications of genetic testing for the access to health care insurances;
- analyse the moral issues of genetic monitoring, genetic screening for predispositions to occupational diseases and genetic testing for prediction of nonoccupational diseases.

PRIVATE AND SOCIAL INSURANCE

A) Private insurance:

• life insurance
• pension insurance
• private health insurance
• private disability insurance

Private insurances are characterised by private liability of the insurance company which runs a financial risk by insuring persons who might make financial claims because of unexpected events like sickness, injury or untimely death. Private insurance companies try to reduce these risks by gathering information on the applicant, particularly if the insured sum is high or the applicant is at high risk of contracting a disease.

B) Social/national insurance:

• national health insurance
• social disability insurance
• state pension schemes

Social or national insurance systems or insurance schemes are based on the responsibility of society to protect the interests of its members against the vicissitudes of life, such as illness, bad luck or old age. These insurances are particularly meant for more vulnerable persons, like people on lower incomes or at higher risks (e.g., of chronic diseases). In some countries, particularly on the European Continent, these national insurances are based on the principles of solidarity and equality. These principles exclude the use of (medical) risk or income as a criterion for access to the insurance.

Genetics and Insurance

With regard to insurances, one may think of life insurance, pension insurance, disability insurance and health insurance. We will start with the use of genetic tests in the context of private life insurance and pension insurance and then move on to the use of genetics in the context of health insurance.

Let us look at a case that was presented by the Helpdesk Health, Work and Insurance of the Dutch Platform for the Insured and Work.

> A woman calls with the following question: 'In view of a number of diseases in my family I have undergone a medical examination some time ago. The result of the examination was that I am a carrier of a gene that increases the susceptibility for breast cancer. At the moment I have no complaints. I am making an application for a mortgage based on a life insurance and I do not know how to fill in the health forms, for example under the heading 'family history'. How should I answer the question 'Have you consulted a specialist in the past five years?' Which consequences might this information have for me? This does not only regard myself, but also my descendants. Suppose that the insurance company keeps a precise record of all the applications and my daughter wants to make an application for life insurance in twenty years time? She may get into trouble at that time, because she has a 50 percent chance to have the gene.
>
> Let us move the case a bit further. Suppose that a woman called Mary Frost is in the same situation. She is filling in a form for an application for a life insurance with Life Invest and is asked whether she has visited a specialist in the past five years. Like the woman in the case above she has consulted a clinical geneticist about possible genetic susceptibility for breast cancer. She also has a daughter, whom she wants to protect. She is very worried about how to answer the question: should she be honest and tell the company that she has consulted a geneticist or should she be silent about it? If she discloses the information, she could be denied the life insurance. Moreover, her children could get into trouble as they could be denied important insurances as a result of the information that she discloses to the insurance company.
>
> Suppose that Mary has a friend, Paul Marks, who works for Global Life, a large insurance company that sells all kinds of private insurances including life insurances. She asks Paul what she should do. Paul is a bit hesitant, because he is not supposed to give advice against the interests of the insurance company. He decides to explain to her in a neutral way the interest to the insurance

company of having medical information, including genetic information, about applicants for a life insurance.

Activity:

How will Paul explain to Mary the interests of an insurance company and the need to obtain all kinds of medical (including genetic) information?

Paul succeeds in convincing Mary that it is better to inform the insurance company that she has consulted a clinical geneticist. Mary completes the form and sends it to Life Invest. Dr Mark Peters, Medical Officer with Life Invest, reads the application form and decides to call Dr Karin Jones, Mary's clinical geneticist, for more information.

Activity:

Suppose you are Dr Karin Jones, and you are called by Dr Mark Peters, asking you to give information on the genetic test of Mary Frost. What will you do? Will you give the information or will you refuse to do so? What are your arguments? Consider for example professional responsibility, duties towards patients and the interests of insurance companies (see above).

If genetic information is used in decisions regarding access to insurance, there will often be a conflict between the applicant and the insurer. In his contribution to the TEMPE workshop on Ethics and Genetics in Milan, Luis Archer made the following comments:

The problem of the access to genetic data from the part of insurance companies is not less difficult than that of the employers. In the case of life, health or other personal insurance, there is a conflict of interests between the insurer and the applicant. On the one hand, the insurer is interested in getting as much information as possible on the genetic predisposition and predictive diseases of the applicant, with the purpose of estimating the true extent of his contractual liability and commensurating premiums with health risks of the applicant. This interest of the insurer is justified by the principle of free enterprise, which allows him to conduct his own business as he sees fit. On the other hand, the applicant is interested in obtaining insurance without having to know or to reveal too many of his/her most intimate weaknesses. This interest is justified by the principle of privacy and by the rights not to know, of nondisclosure and of nondiscrimination.

In favour of the insurer's position of free enterprise are also the social interests of the community, as shown by the fact that, if many predictive tests become easily available and are routinely performed, the cost of the insurance premiums for the individuals with negative results could become considerably lower and this would increase the general access of the public to insurance. Also in favour of the insurer's position is the fact that insurance contracts come under the category of contracts guided by the utmost of good faith. The applicant should inform the insurer of all circumstances known to him which might have a bearing on the assessment of the risk. This is why, in current insurance practice, insurers gather relevant information from the applicants through health questionnaires (family history, etc.) and medical examinations, without general opposition of the applicants. The question only became acute with the prospect of including, in the medical examinations, genetic and predictive tests, which are considered as man's most intimate bastion.

Genetic information

At the end of his contribution, Luis Archer touches upon an important question: what makes genetic information so special? In the past and in current insurance practice, insurers gather relevant medical information through health questionnaires, asking about family history, disease history, etc. The case mentioned above is an illustration of this practice. Sometimes a medical examination is requested. Insurers have done so and are doing so without much general opposition by the applicants or society. We generally acknowledge the right of insurers to gather medical information, particularly in the case of private insurances. Contrary to the so-called social insurances (national health service, state pension schemes, or unemployment benefit), these insurances can be considered a contract between two parties. The insurer has the right to know the risks of the contract and may ask the applicant to reveal all necessary information. On the basis of this information, the insurer can make a risk assessment involved in the contract and calculate the insurance premium. Nobody can expect insurers to insure a 'burning home'. The insurers may argue that genetic information gives them a better prediction of the health risks of an applicant, which enables them to make a better calculation of the premium. This may be an advantage, not only for the insurers, but also for some of the insured. People who on the basis of a genetic test are predicted to pose a low health risk may have their premium reduced. Apart from considerations of justice and solidarity ('why should the victims of the genetic lottery bear its full brunt?'), the idea of a more precise assessment of health risks on the basis of genetic tests is based on a very simplistic idea of the predictive power of genetic information. Though for *some* diseases one can predict with certainty the onset of the disease (like Huntington's disease), for many others one cannot. Tests for heart disease or cancer, for example, are not very accurate, as these diseases are often susceptible to environmental factors and the lifestyle or health behaviour of the applicant. One could then argue that, as the predictive value of genetic knowledge is generally low or moderate, there is no specific difference from other kinds of medical information.

However, there is one big difference between genetic and other medical information, which is the fact that genetic information is not confined to the individual applicant. The information has important consequences for the family of the applicant as well. Insurance companies have always shown great interest in the family history of applicants. Genetic testing may give them a powerful tool to get insight not only in the genetic heritage of the applicant, but also in the genetic heritage of his or her family. Future applications of family members and other relatives may be seriously frustrated by the information insurers have stored about one individual applicant. This may particularly disadvantage persons with a genetic disposition with a high certainty of contracting a disease. Yet also persons with less certain genetic predictions may be disadvantaged, as insurance companies often base their decisions on rough and simplistic ideas about genetic predictions.

The rights of the individual

One of the questions regarding the social use of genetic information is whether the individual can be *forced* to undergo a genetic test. One could argue that the insurer has the right to receive all the necessary information from the applicant in order to make a precise calculation of the risks. But does this include the use of power or pressure? The *Convention on Human Rights and Biomedicine* (Council of Europe 1996) forbids such a use in very explicit terms in Article 12:

> Insofar as predictive genetic testing, in the case of employment or private insurance contracts, does not have a health purpose, it entails a disproportionate interference in the rights of the individual to privacy. An insurance company will not be entitled to subject the conclusion or modification of an insurance policy to the holding of a predictive genetic test. Nor will it be able to refuse the conclusion or modification of such a policy on the ground that the applicant has not submitted to a test, as the conclusion of a policy cannot reasonably be made conditional on the performance of an illegal act.

In many countries there is a strong opposition against the request for predictive testing by insurers. This opposition is generally based on the argument that competent individuals should be free to decide whether they wish to know their genetic status (British Medical Association 1998). The right not to know should be respected and safeguarded. This means that genetic testing should always be based on the consent of the individual.

Let us consider the argument of Luis Archer:

The reluctance of the applicant in being tested or revealing information of genetic nature is justified by the right not to know, by the freedom of decision concerning what personal information should be disclosed, to whom and when, and by the right of not being discriminated. The respect for the right not to know, especially in the so sensitive area of predictive genetics, having profound psychological –emotional impact on the affected persons, is generally accepted and, therefore, the right not to undergo predictive tests should prevail against the interests of the insurer.

Activity:

The right not to know has the aim to protect the interests of the individual. However, we have seen that genetic information does not only affect the individual, but also has implications for other persons, for example family members, social groups or the society at large. Can you give an example of the tension between the right not to know of an individual and the interests of other persons? Can you describe the possible tension between the right not to know and the interests of an insurance company by giving a specific example?

In the Netherlands the Law on Medical Examinations (Wet Medische Keuringen 1997) states that nobody may be tested for untreatable diseases, as such a test is an infringement on the right not to know of the applicant.

Activity:

Reflect for a moment on the Dutch Law. Does the right not to know always outweigh the interests of the insurance company? Or are there cases (for example certain diseases) when the interests of the insurer prevails over the right not to know of the individual?

The right not to know is not the only argument against compulsory predictive genetic testing. As a general rule, in case of predictive genetic testing individuals should always be offered genetic counselling. Insurance companies generally do not have proper facilities for counselling nor appropriate information. This task will be passed on to health care professionals, particularly genetic counsellors. In case of a positive result, the applicant suddenly becomes a client for clinical genetic support. This was not his or her intention when applying for insurance. In general, people expect the results of the test to be negative. A positive result may do serious harm by confronting them with information they prefer not to know.

Because of the strong opposition against predictive genetic testing for insurance purposes, many countries have enacted legislation against this use of genetic testing. For example in France and Germany, national governments have enacted a moratorium in relation to the request for genetic testing for insurance purposes. Such a moratorium was also enacted in the Netherlands, but has been replaced by the Law on Medical Examinations (1997). This Law gives insurers the right to ask questions about medical information, for example on AIDS and genetic information, when the insured sum is to exceed a certain amount (see next section). In the United Kingdom, where the regime of insurance regulations is relatively light, a moratorium is enacted by the insurers themselves, the ABI (Association of British Insurers). In its code of practice the ABI has stated that applicants will not be asked to undergo a genetic test in order to obtain insurance. However, a moratorium only lasts a number of years. It is possible that insurers, because of new developments in the field of genetic testing, will begin to exert political pressure to change the moratorium or to stipulate exceptions to it.

Although there is a consensus at this moment that applicants cannot be requested to undergo predictive genetic testing, it is less clear how one should proceed with *existing* genetic information. Here, the dilemmas are much more difficult and answers are not easy to give. The medical records of applicants may contain information about a positive presymptomatic genetic test or a test for predisposition to a particular disorder. The existing rule in many countries is that all relevant medical information should be disclosed to the insurance company, particularly in the case of private insurance, like life insurance, pension insurance and private health insurance.

Activity:

Let us go back to Dr Mark Peters, Medical Officer of Life Invest. Mark has read the medical history of Mary Frost and has the suspicion that she might have a higher genetic susceptibility to breast cancer. Dr Karin Jones, Mary's clinical geneticist, refuses to give information about the results of the test that Mary underwent a few years ago. Should Mark advise to deny Mary the insurance, because of her reluctance to disclose the test results?

One of the main problems with disclosing existing genetic information is that it might discourage people from undergoing genetic testing with the aim to improve their health status. Most of the genetic information indicates a *risk* of a disease. The actual onset of the disease generally depends on environmental factors, which can be influenced by medication or lifestyle. An example of medication is the use of statines in the case of familiar hypercholesterolaemia. In fact, by genetic testing individuals could become a lower risk to insurance companies, as they may reduce the risk of disease by a healthy lifestyle. (On the other hand one should be aware that such a lifestyle could also be requested by the insurer, which raises new ethical questions.) However, these benefits may be lost when people are discouraged from taking genetic tests out of fear that the results may be used to discriminate against them in case of future insurance applications. Though predictive genetic testing may benefit people, the obligation to disclose this information when applying for insurance may do them serious harm. In view of the principle of nonmalificence, which is one of the governing principles in biomedical ethics, the request for disclosure of existing genetic information may be considered unethical.

Activity:

Is the insurance company's request to disclose genetic information unethical? Insurers cannot be expected to insure a 'burning house'. How should their interests be respected and safeguarded?

The same disadvantage can be noted with regard to genetic counselling in the context of reproductive choices. Prospective parents who want to make informed reproductive choices may be frustrated in their needs, because they fear exclusion from future insurances. People who want to be responsible parents may be punished because of the commercial use of genetic information. Not only are the individuals who are directly involved disadvantaged: these persons might be less inclined to pass genetic information on to their relatives as this information may diminish their chances of gaining access to insurances. This will increase the health risk of their relatives and offspring.

Legal issues

In many countries the legal ban on the use of genetic information for insurance purposes includes existing genetic information. This is, for example, the case in Belgium and the Netherlands. The Belgian Law of Insurance Contracts was passed in 1992. Article 5 of this law states that:

> 'The policy holder is obliged to declare exactly, at the time of completing the contract, any particulars known to him or her which he or she could reasonably be expected to consider as constituting risk assessment elements for the insurer... Genetic data cannot be transmitted.' (McGleenan, 2000: 45–49).

In the Netherlands this legal ban is enacted to enable people to undergo predictive genetic testing by their own free will. However, in the Netherlands the interests of insurance companies are taken into account by establishing a 'ceiling' to the insured sum. In January 2001, this ceiling was an amount of 145.385 euros (Fl. 321.300,00). This sum was laid down in the Medical Examinations Law of 1997 (which replaced the moratorium that was enacted in 1990). Genetic information of applicants will not be sought for sums assured below this amount:

> A proposer cannot be asked about hereditary, untreatable or serious diseases unless the symptoms of these diseases are already manifest. If the sum assured exceeds that stated then the insurer may ask for the results of any genetic test that has already been taken. However, the insurer cannot require an individual to actually take a genetic test. (McGleenan, 2000).

Though the rights of applicants (and his or her health as well as the health of his or her relatives) may be safeguarded by such a ceiling, one could argue that persons in whom a disease has already manifested itself are treated differently from persons who have the same defect but without the disease having manifested itself.

Activity:

Consider this argument. Are tested individuals discriminated against compared to non-tested individuals? Is this an offence against the principle of justice?

One could interpret the 'discrimination' as another argument in favour of requested testing: individuals in equal circumstances (genetic defect) should be treated equally, which is an important principle of justice. However, it is the general opinion that the rights of self-determination and the principle of 'do not harm' (nonmalificence) outweigh the argument of justice.

In case there is no ban on the use of genetic information or the insured sum is higher than the 'ceiling', health care professionals may be asked to pass this information to the insurance companies. However, passing on genetic information, like any other medical information, is bound by the strict rules of confidentiality and privacy. One of the governing principles in medical practice is that health professionals are not allowed to pass (medical) information to third parties without the explicit consent of the individual concerned. Only in case of increased risk to other individuals (for example in the case of HIV-patients) there may be exceptions to this rule. Not only the general practitioner, but also the examining physician should abide by the rule of confidentiality. The Medical Officer of the insurance company has the same duty to preserve the confidentiality of the information of the applicant and his relatives. Insurance companies have a tradition to share information, and particularly in the era of the 'electronic highway', there are real dangers of disclosing confidential information without the client's explicit consent. So, the consent to the disclosure of information not only includes the examining physician, but the Medical Officer as well.

ETHICS AND LAW

It is important to be aware of the differences between ethics and law. Though both disciplines generally share a normative approach to specific issues, there are some important differences between them. Ethics for example is a pluralistic discipline: there are many ethical opinions and arguments, all of which claim to be true. Consequently, the ethical debate is very lively and never 'finished'. On the contrary, the law has to find a common understanding on particular normative issues that can serve as a basis for legal rules. For example the rule of informed consent in many legal documents is based on a shared understanding of the importance of individual autonomy and the right to decide about one's own body. The law must search for such shared meanings and legal rules based on it, in order to regulate the behaviour of individuals and to protect the interests of individuals, for example the interests of vulnerable groups in society, such as people with a higher genetic susceptibility. One cannot impose ethical opinions or arguments on individuals, but one can do so with legal rules. So, while ethics is more or less 'free floating', law is binding and can sanction people who are violating the rules.

Because of the power of the law to regulate normative issues, it is often thought that as soon as we have a legal rule, we no longer need ethics. Ethics is seen as an important step towards the enactment of a legal rule, but loses its relevance as soon as the law has been enacted. However, this is a very narrow view on the role of ethics. Very often the law is very general and needs to be specified when put into practice. For example, if one needs to inform patients about participation in research, how much information does one give them? The Dutch Law on Human Experimentation states that the risks of participation in research need to be outweighed by the benefits: what counts as a benefit and what as a risk? How much weight should be attributed to the risk or to the benefits?

Moreover, legal rules are not flexible and can get outdated in respect of specific issues. They need to be evaluated and adjusted in the light of their effects on (medical) practice. Ethics plays an important role in the evaluation of legal rules and laws, particularly in health care, which is a continuously developing area in our society. Ethics can point to possible negative effects of a law. An example is the Law on Psychiatric Treatment in the Netherlands which states that patients can only be admitted on the basis of their consent, unless they pose a danger to themselves or their surroundings. As a consequence of this law many psychiatric patients are not admitted to psychiatric hospitals because they refuse to give consent, even when they are in need of treatment (but are not in danger or do not represent a danger to others). Many psychiatric patients 'roam the streets' who from a medical viewpoint should be admitted to a hospital.

Ethics can also have a critical function with regard to imposed rules, for instance European rules that do not fit with the dominant ethical viewpoints in a European country. For example, there is much concern in some countries about specific sections of the European Convention, such as the participation of incompetent or minor patients in medical experiments.

Thus both ethics and law are normative disciplines, but have a different character and function in society. Even if we have a legal rule, the ethical debate has not died out. Moreover, ethics can have a critical function with regard to existing or imposed legal rules.

Activity:

You can see from the text in the box above that ethics and law have a different approach and status with respect to normative issues. Could you give an example of the differences between ethics and law in the use of genetic information with regard to access to insurances?

Interpretation

The following section may clarify the need for ethical interpretation of legal rules.

As mentioned above, there is a tendency among insurers to interpret genetic information as a certain predictor of the onset of specific diseases instead of considering them merely as a risk factor. Though for some diseases predicting the (late) onset of a disease is to a certain extent possible, with the majority of genetic defects the disease will only manifest itself in combination with environmental factors (multifactorial diseases).

Guido de Wert reports the following case:

> In the Netherlands, the Law on Medical Examinations (1997) excludes the use of genetic information from previous genetic tests for insurance purposes. However, these legal measures do not prevent problems for persons who make an application for insurance. For example, persons who are carriers of familiar hypercholosterolaemia (FH) have difficulty obtaining life insurance, even if the insured sum is below the ceiling of 145.385 euros. Sometimes, insurance companies do not specifically ask for genetic information on FH, but they do ask whether there has been FH within the family. Thus genetic information can also be used indirectly. In a Dutch study about the use of information on FH, twenty applicants for insurance mentioned on their application form that there was a family history of FH. This was, in their view, medical information which they ought not to conceal from the insurer.

This case not only shows that legal measures do not exclude the indirect use of genetic information, but it also shows the lack of competence within insurance companies to interpret genetic information. FH can be treated very effectively with medication (statines) which will reduce the risk of heart disease. Genetic information on FH (by testing or family history) is no reason to exclude people with this disease from insurance.

Another example is the misinterpretation of the carrier status of individuals. Insurance companies in the United States, for example, have refused life and health insurances to people with a positive test for carrier status, not knowing that the disease would not affect the carrier (British Medical Association 1998). In the United Kingdom, the ABI has perceived the lack of competence among its members regarding the interpretation of genetic information and has appointed a clinical geneticist as an advisor.

Justice

Thus far we have dealt with access to private insurance such as life insurance and pension insurance. Health insurance may also be a private insurance, but in many European countries this is not, or only partly, the case. In some countries, like the United Kingdom, the health care system is not based on insurance, but on free access to a National Health Service (NHS). In many countries access to health care is considered a fundamental right that should not be dependent on the rules and interests of the market place.

JUSTICE AND SOLIDARITY

Health care systems of many European countries are based on the principle of solidarity which means in practice that the 'strong' (that is people with high incomes and/or low health risks) support the 'weak' (that is people with low incomes and/or high health risks) with regard to access to health insurance. Solidarity is, to some extent, an instrumental value in so far as it tries to guarantee equal access to health care for all citizens, irrespective of their income or health risk. This means that people at high risk for genetic disease should have the same access to health services as people at low risk for such diseases.

Equal access to health care could also be based on the principle of justice as, for example, it has been formulated by Aristotle. According to Aristotle, persons who are equal should be treated equally, while persons who are unequal should be treated differently. Important are the criteria according to which persons are considered to be equal. As a general rule people should not be treated differently on the basis of criteria that they cannot influence or determine, like race, sex and physical or mental disabilities. Genetic factors could be included in this list of criteria, as people are born with a specific genetic constitution.

Activity:

Only a small part of the genetic factors result directly in the onset of a disease. Many others are dependent on environmental circumstances and the lifestyle of individuals. Should persons with a genetic predisposition to a disease be treated differently if they do not follow a specific lifestyle or display specific healthy behaviour? For example, if people with FH can prevent heart disease by medication, diet and not smoking, should they be denied access to insurance in case they are smokers? Should health insurers (public or private) have the right to control the lifestyle of people with genetic diseases?

The principle of solidarity in health care confirms the importance of health in our lives. Health and health care are fundamental to fulfil our potential in society and private life. The fundamental importance of health care is the main reason for the special moral status of health insurance. More than life insurance or pension insurance, which are less fundamental provisions, health insurance should not be conditioned on genetic information.

One could ask the question whether genetic testing should be prohibited for *all* health insurances. For example, in the Netherlands only 65 percent of the population is insured with the national health insurance (sickness fund). This national insurance is based on income and risk solidarity. The remaining 35 percent (people above a specific income level) are privately insured. This private insurance is not based on income or risk solidarity. The Dutch Law on Medical Examinations does prohibit genetic testing for life insurance and pension insurance, but not for private health insurance. This may cause problems for people who have undergone genetic testing in the past, and who are now making an application for a private health insurance.

The Helpdesk Health, Work and Insurance of the Dutch Platform for the Insured and Work reports the following case:

> A woman without health complaints wants to be included in the policy of her husband's private health insurance. The insurance company refuses her request. After a telephone inquiry, it appears that in the past she has undergone genetic testing for breast cancer and that this is the reason for being refused by the insurer.

Activity:
Should the use of genetic information be prohibited for all health insurance or only for a specific class of health insurances like sickness funds or the national health service?

The relevance of this question becomes clear in view of the increasing privatisation of health insurance in Europe. As a result of the scarcity of resources, national governments are trying to reduce the level of care of the basic benefit package and are restricting access to services of the health care system.

The accessibility of some health care services to those insured with a sickness fund may be threatened by specific measures such as the transference of benefits to supplementary voluntary insurance, which may lead to inequalities between those insured with a sickness fund and the privately insured. If this trend continues, supplementary insurance will increase its share of the health care costs, which means that there will be a shift from collective to private responsibility. If the use of genetic information is not prohibited in private health insurance, as is the case in the Netherlands, the access to health services may be threatened for an increasing number of citizens.

Privatisation is not only taking place in health insurance but also in disability insurance and other social insurances. National governments are 'retreating' from the social arena to make room for market forces and individual (instead of collective) financial responsibility. Though this operation may facilitate free choice and might decrease bureaucratic control, it may also threaten the opportunities of people with high genetic risks, even if they are not explicitly tested for their genetic constitution.

Activity:

In view of the increasing emphasis in many European countries on individual financial responsibility for protection against the risks of life, should insurance companies take over the collective responsibility of society? Are their limits to the responsibility of the insurer? If there is a new responsibility of the insurers, should they be allowed to make use of genetic information?

The scarcity of resources may also result in limited solidarity within society. For example in the Netherlands, the level of support for the principles of solidarity and equal access is dropping. As appears from public values studies, a significantly larger proportion of the Dutch population now believes that it would be too costly to grant everyone the right to all medical treatments possible. Also less people are prepared to pay higher premiums in order to keep an extensive benefits package available to all (Ter Meulen and Van der Made 2000). This development may result in a decrease in solidarity with persons with specific diseases, particularly diseases that can be attributed to unhealthy or risky behaviour. This process may seriously affect persons with a genetic inheritance, which in combination with environmental circumstances or health behaviour may lead to the onset of specific diseases.

Genetics and the Workplace

A second important use of genetic information is the use of this kind of information by employers for selecting personnel. The ethics of genetic testing in the workplace has to be discussed in terms of the balance between the interests and rights of the employers, of the employees and of society.

According to Luis Archer three main kinds of genetic testing may be considered: genetic monitoring, genetic screening for predispositions to occupational diseases and genetic testing for prediction of nonoccupational diseases.

1. Genetic monitoring of workers tries to assess the possible genotoxic effects of substances or conditions present in the workplace

This genetic monitoring is in the interest of worker's health, of the employer's duty for safety at work, as well as of society's right to health. This testing should be mandatory, if justified. However, if a worker, after being fully informed, denies his/her free consent for the testing, this has to be respected and the job should not be denied for that reason.

It is ethically required that the biological materials obtained from the workers for these health monitoring tests are not used for other genetic testing and are destroyed as soon as the monitoring results are obtained.

In case of a generalised positive result of this genetic monitoring, showing deleterious effects of the working environment, the employer is ethically bound to improve the safety conditions in the workplace.

However, it may happen that only a fraction of the working population is affected by their exposure to the workplace due to the presence of genes causing predisposition or susceptibility to occupational diseases. This can be preventively assessed by independent bodies.

2. *Genetic screening for predispositions to occupational diseases*

It is possible today to identify genes responsible for a predisposition or susceptibility to certain diseases. This means that a given person has a probability, higher than that of the general population, for contracting a certain disease, depending however on environment and living conditions. There are working environments that can cause mutations originating a genetic disease only in the fraction of the population that is genetically susceptible.

It is important to identify the workers possessing such genetic predispositions, so as to avoid their access to specific posts involving greater risk. This limitation in their right to work is justified by their right to health. But even in such cases, the testing should be performed on a voluntary basis, under conditions of a fully informed and free consent. If a worker refuses to undergo this test, his or her contract should nevertheless remain in force.

In these cases, it is important that the disease keeps being considered as occupational, since, in fact, its agent is environmental. This form of genetic testing should not be allowed to slip into detection of hereditary diseases in general and lead to discrimination. Even more important is to avoid a selection of resistant workers with the purpose of saving the expenses connected with physical improvements of the working conditions. It would be greatly unjust to accept lower levels of safety at the cost of the exclusion of part of the working population.

The rights of society to health should also be considered. There are certain jobs in which the unexpected deterioration of the worker's health could affect the safety of the public or of the fellow workers. A typical example is that of an airline pilot.

In these cases, predictive tests (as, for instance, detecting a gene predisposing an individual to a sudden heart attack under conditions of changing oxygen pressure) may help to prevent serious accidents and are ethically justified. However, there is a danger of overgeneralising this principle and using these predictive tests with unjustified frequency. For instance, there are no ethical reasons to justify the exclusion of a person with the gene for Huntington's chorea from being a pilot, as long as he/she is healthy. Regulations and provisions should be made in order to create independent bodies with the task of restricting the requirement of predictive tests for safety reasons to reasonable proportions and defending the rights of potential or real workers no less than society's rights to safety.

This ethical position is in accordance with the Convention on Human Rights and Biomedicine of the Council of Europe (Council of Europe 1997) in its Article 12 where we read:

> Article 12 prohibits the carrying out of predictive tests for reasons other than health or health-related research, even with the assent of the person concerned. Therefore, it is forbidden to do predictive genetic testing as part of preemployment medical examinations, whenever it does not serve a health purpose of the individual. This means that in particular circumstances, when the working environment could have prejudicial consequences on the health of the individual because of a genetic predisposition, predictive genetic testing may be offered without prejudice to the aim of improving working conditions. The test should be clearly used in the interest of the individual's health. The right not to know should also be respected.

Activity:

Do employers have the right to decide about employing a person if a person agrees to participate in screening and is found to be at increased risk for a specific job?

According to the philosopher John Harris (1992) the risk will be slight and many detected persons will not succumb to it. It seems unreasonable automatically to exclude all those who show an increased susceptibility. If the individual chooses to accept this risk and to embark on the job, there could be strong reasons to prevent him or her from doing so. On the basis of this argument, the British Medical Association (1995) says the following:

> In our society the principle of self-determination is held in high esteem: individuals should be free to accept certain risks, providing they are informed of the implications and the decision does not put others, who have not consented, at risk. Where other people, such as other employees or members of the public, would be put at risk by the individual's decision, there might be grounds for overruling that decision.

In case of unreasonable risks, individuals should be defended against themselves. However, it is difficult to tell what risk or harm should be classified as unreasonable.

Let us look at the third area of genetic testing in relation to work, as mentioned by Luis Archer:

3. Genetic testing for prediction of non-occupational diseases

It is possible to detect genes responsible for late-onset diseases that are independent from workplace conditions, but are incapacitating. Through these tests it is possible to predict, several years or even decades ahead of time, specific diseases, many of which are, so far, incurable.

Although such diseases are nonoccupational, employers are interested in obtaining the results of these tests, in order to ascertain the possibility of premature incapacitation of the applicants for a job. In fact, employers are supposed to reduce production costs and increase cost effectiveness of investments. For this purpose they have to avoid inefficiency or absenteeism of the worker, loss of the training investment caused by premature incapacitation of the employee and increased costs for health, disability or death insurance contributions.

These interests of the employers are legitimate. In the framework of a market economy that accepts the free enterprise system, the employers have the duty of safeguarding productivity and looking for the best return on their investments. Nevertheless, these legitimate interests must be weighed against the equally legitimate interests of the workers and of society.

The workers have several interests and rights, such as the right to autonomous decision and informed consent, the right not to know, the right to maintain health, to protect privacy, the right to not being discriminated against on the basis of genetic characteristics and the right to work, which is a fundamental element of many modern constitutions and international agreements (Sola 1995). Work is a necessity for personal fulfilment and integration in society, in addition to being, to the vast majority of the population, the main source of income and sustenance. To deny employment for reasons not of incapacity but of a mere prediction of a future disease would represent unfair discrimination. This would be even more unjust than the denial to disabled persons of the special protection, laid down in most laws, for the enjoyment of their right to work.

Access to work should not be denied because of the prediction of a disease. Otherwise a class of people would be created who, although currently fit for work, are barred from employment. This discrimination is unjust for the individual and burdensome for society. These persons would have to be supported by public funds and estimations have shown that they would cost more to society than they would to the employer.

Activity:

Stop here for a moment: is it the responsibility of the individual employer to meet the needs of disabled people, even if this may ruin his financial position?

According to Luis Archer the interests of the individual employee take precedence:

> For all these reasons, the dominant ethical position is that the interests of the worker, in such cases, should take precedence over the interests of the employer and that the latter is only allowed to inquire about the present, but not the future, health conditions of a job applicant. In summary, the exclusion of people from employment opportunities based on genetic testing seems to be ethically acceptable only when proven to be absolutely necessary for the worker's health or for the safety of a third party (Nairne 1995).

> The UNESCO Universal Declaration on the Human Genome and the Human Rights sets out, in article 6, that 'No one shall be subjected to discrimination based on genetic characteristics that is intended to infringe or has the effect of infringing human rights, fundamental freedoms and human dignity' (UNESCO Universal Declaration on the Human Genome and the Human Rights, 1997). More recently, the Final Report of the United States Task Force on Genetic Testing stated: 'No individual should be subjected to unfair discrimination by a third party on the basis of having had a genetic test or receiving an abnormal genetic test result. Third parties include insurers, employers and educational and other institutions that routinely inquire about the health of applicants for services or positions. Discrimination can take the form of denial or of additional charges for various types of insurance, employment jeopardy in hiring and firing, or requirements to undergo unwanted genetic testing' (Holtzman and Watson 1998).

Again, this is quite a restrictive policy for employers. Although it seems based on quite sound arguments, you may try to highlight some contextual features of the situation: employers would probably look for ways to protect themselves from hiring prospectively diseased workers, notwithstanding laws and rules proscribing explicit discrimination. Should we look for stricter rules (on the basis on the non-negotiability of rights to autonomy and privacy) or should we balance the various interests at stake (on the basis of a cost-benefit analysis such as that suggested by utilitarianism)? Some of you may even want to put forward some arguments in favour of the interests of the employers.

In case predictive screening is allowed, the employers should take care to interpret the information correctly. The British Medical Association (1998) is quite clear about this:

> If employers do not have the relevant expertise to understand the implications of a positive genetic test there is a risk that all people who have a positive test may be excluded from employment, even if they are carriers and are, themselves, unaffected. General practitioners should therefore give detailed information about the practical implications of the individual's genetic status and, possibly, suggest that more detailed information is sought from the geneticist responsible for the individual's care. Occupational health physicians receiving pre-employment medical reports showing a positive genetic test should seek specialised advice about the implications of the result before making decisions or providing advice to the employer about the individual's application.

The potential benefits of genetic tests to employers will always have to be balanced against the interests of the employee and of society. The possible harms to the employee and the right to self-determination will generally outweigh the advantages of such tests to the employer.

Summary

In this chapter we dealt with:
- the role of genetic information in decisions on access to social goods, particularly insurances and the workplace;
- the special character of genetic information compared to 'normal' medical information in respect with the application for insurances;

- the (non)acceptability of requesting applicants to undergo a genetic test or to supply genetic information from past tests;
- the difference between the legal and the ethical approach in the access to genetic information;
- the role of genetic information and the principle of solidarity in the access to health care insurance;
- the role of genetic information in the selection of personnel;
- the screening of employees for genetic predispositions for occupational diseases and nonoccupational diseases.

We have analysed and discussed the social use of genetic information by way of cases, for example, the problem of disclosing genetic information from previous tests when applying for a life insurance. What are the obligations and responsibilities in such a situation of the clinical geneticist? We have also looked at legal regulations in various European countries and at the European Convention. By way of practical exercises we have explained the difference between ethics and law as well as issues of justice with respect to access to care. We have underlined the problem of uncertainty in respect to genetic information and the impossibility of basing hard decisions on it. The ethical issues of genetic testing and the workplace were discussed and explained by reference to several international and national documents, including the UNESCO Declaration on the Human Genome and the Human Rights and the position of the British Medical Association.

Are We Our Genes?

In the debate on the ethical implications of genetics, the question is always raised whether genetic information should be considered as a special kind of medical information and even whether it calls for a paradigm shift in ethics. In fact, a number of arguments might support both the exceptionalist and the nonexceptionalist position. Even though it is becoming increasingly difficult to distinguish among different kinds of relevant sensitive personal data, and boundaries between genetic and other medical information are blurred, genetics raises specific issues. In this chapter we will reflect on two of those issues:

● the relation between the individual and the community in the context of genetic testing, screening and research;
● the various levels of predictability of genetic factors and the issues of genetic determinism.

Objectives

After reading this chapter you will be able to:

● understand from a philosophical viewpoint the relation between the individual and community in the context of genetic testing, screening and research;
● assess the moral implications of the various levels of predictability of genetic factors;
● analyse the issue of genetic determinism and personal identity from a philosophical viewpoint;
● understand the importance of fundamental issues, like the role of genetics in individual lives.

From Individuals to Community

In Chapter 1 and 2 the relational dimension of genetic information has been pointed out. Because of their genetic
make-up, individuals are linked with each other, not only
within families but also in larger communities and populations. This means that genetic data cannot be merely
considered as, and reduced to, a matter of individuality (individual choice and privacy).

Shifting from genetic testing to genetic screening causes the
widely accepted and relatively unquestioned principle of
autonomy to become increasingly problematic, for different
reasons. On the one hand, the individualistic approach
prevailing in contemporary medical ethics is, if not relativised,
partially inadequate vis-à-vis the community assessment of
genetic information that is not exclusively owned but shared
among different people. On the other hand, the risk exists for
individuals to merely become the means for implementing
some social health plans.

In decisions on genetic testing, screening and research, one
must always be aware of the interests of the individual and
the interests of other persons who are genetically linked to
him or her. An ethical decision is a decision that tries to
balance the interests of the individual and those of the
community. A genetic research project or screening
programme may harm the interests of an individual. For
example the case of screening for three genetic disorders in
Finland in Chapter 3 is an example of how community interests may harm the interests of the individual. On the other
hand, a decision on testing individuals may have repercus-
sions for family members and relatives. An example is testing
for BRCA gene: when a mother let herself be tested for this
gene, the daughter will be affected by this decision. For
example, she may be denied access to certain kinds of insurance.

In her paper on Genetic Databases, which is part of Chapter
3, Ruth Chadwick wonders whether the existing principles of
medical ethics can deal with the many new issues which are
put forward by genetic research and the banking of genetic
information. In particular in the context of genetic research,
in which individuals are asked for their consent to provide a
sample of their 'genes', the issue of informed consent becomes

highly problematic. One of the important issues, according to Chadwick, is the possible discrimination of individuals and the stigmatisation of certain groups. Informed consent by the individual is not enough to protect his or her interests, nor those of others.

Yet not only in genetic research, but also in access to insurance or to the workplace, informed consent by individuals to earlier testing may have far-reaching implications for their own future or that of their relatives. Does genetics call for a 'paradigm shift' in ethics, with a greater emphasis on the interests of larger groups or communities versus the interests of the individual? Does genetic testing, screening and research pave the way for an alternative approach in ethics, in which communitarian values like solidarity will play a more important role?

'Paradigm shift' here means that the basic assumptions of our moral reasoning are challenged by previously unforeseeable conditions, which make the most commonly and widely accepted moral concepts (individual autonomy, full information and consent, etc.) partially inadequate.

Activity:

Imagine that you are a clinical geneticist offering a genetic test to an individual, for example a test for the BRCA gene. In what way would you take into account the interests of others (like the family, relatives, a social group). Does adopting this wider perspective change your existing view on informed consent?

Shifting from a more individualistic approach to a mostly community-centred one also involves encountering problems that call for an ethical and legal analysis.

Rulemaking on genetics, because of its strong impact on the society as a whole, requires a kind of mix of ethics and the law (see Chapter 4). A great many policies and regulatory documents on genetics already exist due to the fear of potential negative consequences in an unregulated context.

Actually, it is difficult to establish legislation in the field of genetics due to the pace with which developments take place and the difficulty with assessing the social consequences.

It has been suggested that the response of the law should be to monitor rather than to ban, and self-regulation by guidelines or codes of conduct should be preferred to statutory regulation; at an international level, common principles should serve as a common framework for adequate national policies (Chadwick et al. 1998).

Some issues can be regulated at a national level, but international regulations seem to be preferred for several reasons: the development of an international system in genetics, which creates a common responsibility concerning possible harmful consequences. Moreover, it has been recommended that an independent coordinating body be established at an international level to address matters of common interest and standards.

From Predictability to Uncertainty

The probabilistic character of genetic information, the unpredictability and complexity of multifactorial genetic diseases, the controversies about the reliability of some existing tests, and the lack of widely accepted standards for interpreting genetic data make genetic information highly disputable for supporting individual and social decisions.

Even if the same test is used for both screening and diagnostic testing, its predictive value (proportion of persons testing positive who have the condition or testing negative who do not have the condition) will differ. Changes to sensitivity (ability of the test to detect all those who have, or who will develop, the disease), specificity (ability to classify correctly those persons who do not have, or will not develop, the disease), and predictive value of a genetic test occur when moving from a population with a high prevalence to one with a low. This could reflect either a lower prevalence of the disorder and a consequent drop in the positive predictive value of the test or a weaker correlation between genotype and overt disease in the general population due to ascertainment bias in the original population.

In this respect genetics represents a special case of a decision under conditions of uncertainty and should be discussed within the social assessment of risks, uncertainty and ignorance (Smith and Wynne 1989, Jasanoff 1995).

Despite the uncertainty, genetic information is often interpreted under deterministic assumptions on the reliability of its approach. The risks involved in genetic determinism lead to the issues of who is given the power to make decisions, how decision making processes should take place, and what role has to be assigned to public participation in decision making. This determinism is also linked to reductionism, that is the point of view according to which genetics is the ultimate explanatory level.

On the following pages you are not going to deal with a case, but with a paper to read. This paper, written by Ruth Chadwick, raises a number of questions about how gene therapy can affect personal identity and whether it is challenging the notion of 'self' and 'personality'. Though Somatic Gene Therapy and Germ-line Gene Therapy are not the subject of this workbook on clinical genetics, the paper deals with problems that you have already encountered, such as genetic determinism and reductionism, i.e., the possibility that people are considered only as the sum of (the expression of) their genes.

Before you start reading Ruth Chadwick's paper, you are asked to take notice of some initial ethical questions that are raised by Somatic Gene Therapy and Germ-line Gene Therapy.

Does gene therapy (GT) raise new questions?

The development of the Human Genome Project and the subsequent refinement of technological intervention in the human genetic endowment creates the possibility of new and revolutionary treatments: the potentialities of gene therapy, both in the somatic (Somatic Gene Therapy – SGT) and the germ-line cells (Germ-Line Gene Therapy – GLGT), offer prospects of radical treatment for a number of diseases with a genetic basis. The more we know about our genome, the nearer we will get to the time when not only the diagnosis of certain illnesses but also their treatment will be feasible directly at the molecular level.

After the application of SGT on human beings, there has been some criticism about the results achieved so far: these were not as outstanding as expected, and the application of gene therapy to some dreadful diseases, although possible in principle, is yet to come; yet these critiques are based on excessive expectations raised by the media and, partially, by the scientific community itself (an interesting problem of communication management), while research is proceeding at a fast rate towards new applications. Major scientific advances are blurring the borderline between SGT and GLGT: interventions in the genome are being pushed progressively backwards to earlier stages of cell development and differentiation, so that in some instances GT, even if intended to affect only somatic cells, will also inevitably affect germ line cells. This raises serious problems for the ethical assessment of these practices. These problems are not just of a legal, political and practical nature, but mainly of a conceptual and philosophical one: the main difficulties for the international community (scientific and public) in dealing with the application of the new genetics lie in the conceptual untidiness of the words and notions employed to discuss illness, health, therapy and the very image of man.

Up to now, international debate has led to the agreement, expressed for example in the *Opinion of the Group of Advisers on Ethical Implications of Biotechnology of the European Commission* (European Commission 1997), that, since the scientific basis and technical feasibility of germ-line gene therapy are far from being established, 'no proposal for clinical experimentation of germ line gene therapy on humans is at present even contemplated' (1.7), and that – on the other hand – 'somatic gene therapy should be restricted to serious diseases for which there is no other effective treatment' (2.4). Furthermore, the *Convention for the Protection of Human Rights in Biomedicine* (Council of Europe 1997), affirms that 'an intervention seeking to modify the human genome may only be undertaken if its aim is not to modify the genetic characteristics of descendants and only for preventive, diagnostic or therapeutic purposes' (Art. 13).

These statements already represent a good enough guideline for present research in the field. Yet it is important to notice their use of words and the key concepts that sustain their plausibility: 1) they are based on the distinction between *somatic* gene therapy and germ line gene therapy, and 2) they imply a clearly defined distinction between prevention, diagnosis and therapy on the one side and enhancement on the other.

Recent developments, both in the technical aspects and in the ethical and philosophical debate concerning genetics, lead to questioning these distinctions: the borders between somatic and germ-line gene therapy, as well as between therapy and enhancement of health, are becoming even more vague in terms of conceptual tidiness, practical relevance and normative value, so that if we fail to clarify those distinctions and the underlying concepts, the existing consensus will vanish and the guidelines will lose their meaning. Gene therapy forces us to build a more flexible and clear consensus, so that the challenges posed by these new technologies can be faced with a firmer conceptual grip and in a more practical framework. This means that the distinctions and the concepts lying at the basis of present guidelines must be either specified or even abandoned for new ones.

Thus we might summarise the work ahead of those studying the ethical implications of genetic diagnosis and treatment by the following questions:

- Is the current moral language on gene therapy (and more generally on genetic intervention in people) adequate?
- Do we really know what we mean by such terms as 'therapy', 'enhancement', 'disease' and 'health need'?
- What are the main differences between the cultural approaches to gene therapy in different countries? How are those terms understood respectively?
- What are the major difficulties from a scientific, social, legal, ethical and philosophical point of view, to be overcome before application in people can be accepted, if ever? More specifically, the question whether the *moral* distinction between *somatic* and germ-line gene therapy is sound should be posed, and it will be necessary to develop an analysis and a proposal on how to draw this distinction in a useful manner. The same critical analysis should be advanced for the distinction between *therapy* and *enhancement* as a moral guideline for policies. At the moment, both distinctions are criticised from different points of view (scientific and conceptual), yet alternative guidelines have not been developed and would hardly gain sufficient consensus.

The distinction between therapy and enhancement raises even more controversies as it is connected not only with the disputed borders between health and illness, but also with the idea of *human nature*. In fact, in order to say that a certain treatment (let us suppose, a genetic treatment aimed at increasing mnemonic capacities) *enhances* an individual's abilities beyond the normal human range, we need to have a clear idea of what kind of memory a human being is supposed to have (and, again, a purely statistical notion will not suffice here). Also, the more we will be able to intervene in the modification of the genetic patrimony, the more it will become questionable where the borderline is between treating a human being and *changing* him/her into something different.

Paper for discussion

Gene Therapy and Personal Identity
Ruth Chadwick

(Institute for Environment, Philosophy and Public Policy, Lancaster University, UK)

Reprinted from G.K. Becker (ed.), The Moral Status of Persons, Amsterdam-Atlanta, Rodopi, 2000: 183–194.

1. Introduction

A defining feature of gene therapy, in contrast to conventional medical treatment, is that it is explicitly designed to bring about changes at the genetic level, by, for example, introducing a functioning gene into a human being who lacks one. Questions arise as to whether the alteration of an individual's genetic make-up could bring about a change in who that person is, an identity change, and if so whether this is something about which there are grounds for concern from a moral point of view. In order to answer these questions it is necessary to examine what the connection is, if any, between genes and the person, and how that might be affected by gene therapy.

There might be several different ways in which genes and the person could be connected, genes as the 'essence' of the person, or genes as a criterion of identity over time. What some commentators appear to be interested in, however, is a person's *sense* of their own identity. It is important to distinguish these different levels; otherwise the debate about the acceptability of gene therapy is liable to confusion.

2. Am I My Genes?

The debate as to what counts as essentially 'me' is of long-standing – whether, for example, I am my brain; whether the person can be reduced to the combination of physical and mental attributes that make up a person as we experience them; whether there is something over and above this set of attributes. It would be beyond the scope of this discussion to rehearse the arguments for and against competing accounts of the person. Instead, it will be relevant to address the ways in which an account in terms of DNA relates to these debates.

First, a physical account of the person. A standard objection to any physical account of the person, such as that which identifies the person with his or her brain, is the possibility of division and the problem of how to account for that. The suggestion that the essence of the person might consist in their DNA is open to the objections to which a physical criterion is subject. In so far as it has a physical existence – it is material stuff – it can have bits added and removed. Also, whereas the philosophical puzzles generated by the possibility of dividing a brain and transplanting the two halves into different people are thought experiments, we know that the DNA in one fertilised egg can and does split into two when identical twins are formed. This has led to difficulties about establishing when a person's life story begins. Bernard Williams, for example, formulated a Zygotic Principle (ZP) to deal with this question, such that 'a possibility in which a given human being, A, features is one that preserves the identity of the zygote from which A developed' (Williams, 1990). Williams subsequently modified ZP in order to deal with the possibility of monozygotic twinning, so that 'a story is about A if it is about an individual who developed from the earliest item from which A in fact uniquely developed (Williams, 1990').

The brain has had a central place in discussions of personal identity because of its role as the necessary condition of consciousness and mental life, and this has contributed to the importance of psychological criteria, rather than a physical substrate, for the essence of the person. One of the most influential accounts of what it means to be a person has been the view that a person is a being with self-awareness. The idea that we could hold up a disk containing our genetic profile and say 'That's me,' as has been envisaged by some genome scientists (Gilbert 1992), does not take this into account. On the self-awareness account, it is the capacity to give voice to the statement 'That's me' that is crucial, not the information itself. This objection however might not count against a view which gives importance to potentiality. One of the considerations supporting giving moral consideration to embryos and foetuses has been the view that all the genetic information is in place that, other things being equal, will lead to the development of a person, is in one place, as stated in the discussion of the physical criterion above. So in this sense the traditional argument for potentiality supports the view that the genetic information has a crucial role to play. This does not establish, however, that the genes are the person, but only that they constitute a necessary condition for the development of the person and their psychological states.

Perhaps, however, the attraction of DNA as the essence of the person is its candidature for the part of, some fact over and above physical or psychological attributes, that constitutes the essence of the person. This seems to be what is suggested in accounts that put forward DNA as the modern secular equivalent of the soul. Dorothy Nelkin and Susan Lindee, for example, have drawn attention to the parallels between the Christian soul and DNA, which, they suggest, are 'more than linguistic or metaphorical' (Nelkin and Lindee, 1995: 41).

'DNA has taken on the social and cultural functions of the soul. It is the essential entity – the location of the true self – in the narratives of biological determinism' (Nelkin and Lindee, 1995).

It has also taken on the soul's role as the guarantor of immortality. We find a degree of immortality in passing on our genes to our descendants. Cloning offers a vision of passing on all of them instead only half, and thus may appear more attractive to those in search of continued existence. Unlike a soul, however, as we have already seen, DNA has a physical existence. What makes DNA attractive as a soul-like candidate, however, is its double aspect – as both physical stuff and as containing 'information.' Whereas we know that all the cells of the body are replaced over a period of years, in each new replacement cell the nucleus will contain the same set of genes. It is this that makes cloning by somatic cell nuclear transfer a possibility, and which has led to the metaphor of the 'blueprint.' Our DNA, it is said, contains all the information that influences our physical and mental characteristics. The genetic information gathered inside the nucleus governs the future development of an identifiable individual.

There are problems with this account. First, the blueprint metaphor has to be recognised for what it is – a metaphor. The implications of the adoption of this metaphor for our ways of seeing persons have to be acknowledged:

'The expansion of information technologies and communication systems ... have laid the foundations for the formation and validation of different forms of knowledge and new ways of seeing the body and the self'.

And

'In genetics, for example, the body is conceptualised through informational metaphors, broken down into microscopic units which can be reprogrammed (...). The body is seen as a potentially correctly programmed system which, through scientific intervention, might be improved by the replacement of abnormal genes with normal ones' (Stacey 1997).

This way of seeing the person, as a complex information system, competes with other perspectives. Nelkin and Lindee link the genetic perspective with biological determinism, but environmental factors influence both physical characteristics such as stature; and mental attributes such as intellectual achievement. Even if we accept that all the information is contained in the DNA, laying down the potential attributes of the person, environmental factors will affect which parts of that potential are realised. So what does it mean to say that my genes are me, if large parts of my genome will never be activated?

A possible response to this might be that what is important is precisely that my genome endures throughout all environmental changes whether or not parts of it remain inactivated, just as the soul was thought to exist, intact, throughout all the vicissitudes of life. This interpretation could give support to the view that the genes are the essence of the person, which might manifest differently in the phenotype according to environment.

Against this view of genes as the 'essential encoder' Hugh Miller argues for a commonsense view of the person, traced to an Aristotelian account: 'Persons are physical (biological) entities with distinctively rational capacities, or modes of functioning. They are material bodies that can do certain distinctive things' (Miller 1998).

In his view the identity of a person is determined by the character he or she develops as he or she passes through space and time. Miller rejects the idea of an immaterial self such as a Cartesian ego, while wanting to retain the idea of the essence of personhood being linked with both free will and moral responsibility, and with our biological nature. Psychological criteria are therefore central but cannot dispense with attachment to a material body located in space and time. The question then arises: to what extent do genes determine character? Miller argues that there are three possible answers to this, corresponding to different degrees of determinism. His conclusion is that genetically determined traits function as parameters within which a human being is free to develop a unique character which make him or her the person he or she is (Miller 1998). DNA is a necessary condition of personal identity but should not be conflated with it. The rival accounts of the essence of the person as consisting in the genetic blueprint or in the character are thus intricately intertwined with questions of determinism, free will and responsibility.

As Miller has argued, sameness of DNA cannot logically guarantee sameness of person, because otherwise identical twins would be one and the same person and this is not the case. In addition to travelling distinct spatio-temporal paths, they have different life stories and develop different characters, although identical twins, unlike clones, even share the same mitochondrial DNA. Miller further argues, however, that if two organisms of the same species have different DNA blueprints, then it follows from the logic of identity that they must be different persons. But this does not follow unless it is assumed that personhood does exist in the DNA, and Miller argues, as stated above, that while DNA is a necessary condition of personal identity, it should not be conflated with the essential encoder. If this is so it would be important for the consideration of identity over time.

Activity:

Stop for a moment and think about arguments offered here against genetic determinism – the idea that humans are their genes. How can these arguments be employed effectively against social risks of discrimination and exclusion for genetic reasons?

3. Identity Over Time

In accordance with different views on what constitutes the essence of a person, there are associated criteria of identity over time. Depending on the view that is taken on the first question, there will be differences of opinion on how much change can take place, for example in gene therapy, without implying the conclusion that an identity change has taken place.

The use of genetic fingerprinting as a means of identification, to show that the individual being accused at time t2 is one and the same individual as the person who committed the crime at time t1, does not show that DNA is the criterion of identity in a deep sense. Fingerprints, after all, were used as a *means* of identification, but without any suggestion that they constituted the essence of the person.

If personal identity consists in something other than the DNA, then it would in principle be possible to bring about some change at the DNA level, for example by gene therapy, which would not constitute a change in the identity of the person. There are different possibilities: (1) that any change in the DNA brings about an identity change; (2) that a change in a certain proportion brings about an identity change; (3) that a change in a key part brings about an identity change.

(1) will only be the case if 'I' am identical with my complete set of genes. Given the facts, however, that human beings share over 99 percent of their genes, and doubts about whether a gene that is expressed in only one organ can appropriately be called 'human' (Pottage 1998), it seems implausible to accept that *no* change, even in one gene, would be permissible. (2) depends on a physical criterion of personal identity with all the associated problems. (3) depends on the prior question of which aspects of the person are thought to be the *sine qua non,* for example, which psychological attributes or character traits; and if that can be answered, can we identify which genes are associated with the characteristics in question?

4. Gene Therapy

Gene therapy might be supposed to pose a threat to personal identity in so far as the therapy introduces an identity-changing effect (see, for example, Elliott 1993). It is germ-line,

rather than somatic, therapy, however, that is normally considered to be susceptible to this problem. The conceptual
distinction between somatic and germ-line therapy is typically
drawn via the point that while somatic therapy affects the body
cells of an individual, germ-line therapy also affects the reproductive cells, thereby having an impact on that individual's
children and ultimately on the gene pool of the species (see,
for example, Clothier 1992). This attempt to distinguish
between them conceptually has never, however, been entirely
clear-cut. It has for some time been envisaged as a possibility
that cells being introduced into the body in the course of
somatic therapy could recombine with other viruses and infect
the germ cells. *New Scientist* has reported evidence of such
'contamination' (14 March 1998). The proposals for *in utero*
gene therapy has also given rise to speculation about inadver-
tent transfer into germ cells (Schneider and Coutelle 1999).
More radically, the Dolly experience has undermined the
distinction between types of cell. The implication that every
somatic cell is now a potential embryo has led to the necessity
of reexamining our definitions of concepts such as 'embryo.'

Somatic therapy carried out on an adult with informed
consent is commonly considered to be no different in principle from an organ transplant such as the introduction of a
donor kidney (which also contains extraneous genetic material). It is of course true that, especially in the early days,
recipients of donor organs experienced some psychological
problems connected with their sense of identity, but these
have not been construed as challenges to identity in a deep
sense. As Bernard Williams puts it 'In general, "same X which
consists of parts" doesn't entail an X which consists of the
same parts. There's no puzzle about replacement cells'
(Williams 1990), so analogously it would be difficult to
sustain an argument for the view that inhaling a functioning
gene in, for example a nasal spray, as has been tried in the
case of cystic fibrosis, would pose a threat to any essential
core. And adding a functioning gene is what is normally envisaged, although as replacement becomes more common it is
conceivable that this might be thought to make a difference.

In germ-line therapy however, what is under consideration
is therapy to change the genetic constitution of an individual
at the embryonic stage. As such, any change would be global
rather than local, it would not be targeting a particular part

of the body such as the lungs or bone marrow. Whether such an intervention would have an identity-changing effect or not depends, as already indicated, on whether at the embryonic stage we do have a person – whether there is a full 'blueprint' of the individual in the embryo that does in fact constitute the essential identity of that person. Some would argue that what we have at this stage of development is not a person but a potential person. It could still be argued, however, that a genetic intervention at this stage will affect, if not determine, who that individual will be.

There is disagreement here both on the status of the embryo and on the relation between genes and personal identity. In this situation it might be helpful to try another approach and ask whether a future person could legitimately claim to have a grievance as a result of gene therapy performed at the embryonic stage.

5. What Grievances Might a Future Person Have?

One way of addressing this question is to ask what grievances a future person might have. As I have argued elsewhere (Chadwick 1998), in response to Bernard Williams's suggestion that there are only two, namely 'I should have had a nicer time' and 'It would have been better if I had never existed' (Williams 1990), there are other possibilities, including 'I should not have had my genome altered,' 'I should have been someone else,' 'I should have been free of this genetic disorder,' 'I should have been given genetic immunisation' and 'I should not have been brought into existence.' I suggested that those grievances which were coherent presupposed sameness of identity; the grievance which deals explicitly with identity change, namely 'I should have been someone else' is not coherent because, as Williams pointed out, l could not have been someone else; what could have been the case is that I did not exist and someone else did.

This analysis, however, is incomplete, because the grievance may lie elsewhere than in an identity issue of this sort: it may lie instead in the individual's *sense* of their own identity.

The person who says 'I should not have had my genome altered' may have a coherent grievance but not one that lies in a personal identity issue. The statement of the grievance presupposes that identity has been preserved. Nevertheless it may be *perceived* as a personal identity issue.

There are at least two ways in which a person's perception of their identity may be affected. One possible grievance a future person might have is 'I don't know who I am', meaning that he or she does not know what his or her genetic origins were. This issue has been more commonly raised where paternity has been in doubt, but reproductive technology has changed that. In the light of the possibility of reproductive cloning, one question that may be asked is 'Am I a copy?' Why is this important? Given genetic heritage, the individual nevertheless develops in a unique way and also has the potential for what is called self-creation. Concern for genetic origins is, however, still regarded as very important in our society.

Marilyn Strathern (1992) has suggested that this may disappear:

> Perhaps the current interest in genetic origins will turn out to have been more of a radical ... break with the past, and with the old reproductive model, than it is an evolutionary development of what we already know ... I am not so certain that we shall in future need representations of downward inheritance or of relations embodied in relationships: all that we shall need is the program ... . Questions that the individual person once asked of him or herself about origin and links need no longer be asked ... when they can be asked of the individual's genome'.

This in itself, however, is presupposing that identity consists in the genes and not in other factors such as situatedness, which is precisely in dispute.

The second way that a person's perception of their identity may be involved is in so far as they identify themselves with their genes or particular characteristics which they take to be genetic. We see this, for example, in arguments put forward by disability rights organisations in opposition to the new genetics and its attempts to 'cure' conditions which are not regarded as disorders by their possessors. There are at least two separate strands to be disentangled here. The first is the concern that attempts to eliminate or cure genetic conditions will lead to a society less tolerant of disability. This is typically countered by an argument that what is the object of these attempts is not the *people* but the *conditions*. At this point the second strand comes into play, which is that it is not possible to distinguish these two elements, because their identity is dependent upon their genetic condition. Whereas an individual who suffers from a disease such as smallpox can conceptualise themselves without this disease, this is not possible in the case of certain genetic conditions.

The question arises as to whether this is true of all conditions that have a genetic component. In the case of a predisposition to a multifactorial disease, such as breast cancer, the individual concerned may not know of the predisposition, and so her identity has been constructed without this knowledge. It has been argued, therefore, that there may be a right not to know genetic information on the grounds that it may constitute a threat to the individual's sense of their identity (Chadwick et al. 1997). The fact that this argument is put forward for the right not to know that one has a genetic predisposition *on these grounds* supports an argument for the view that one's knowledge about one's genes plays an important part in constructing one's identity in this sense. (Indeed, both origins and predispositions are important in this respect).

The point is, how seriously should we take this as an objection to gene therapy? It is easy enough to make sense of the person who has a grievance that they have been given information which has changed for the worse their perception of their self and their future; but what about the individual who objects to gene therapy to remove deafness on the grounds that it has turned them into a different person? What we have seen above is that if this was an identity change in the deep sense they would not be able to voice this as a coherent grievance. Let us look at what coherent grievances *may* be expressed:

- I am no longer the same person [because my condition played an essential part in constructing my identity].
- An attempt to eliminate my condition constitutes an attack on what is essentially me.
- I am no longer able to regard myself in the same way.

The third is the most straightforward. It draws attention to psychological consequences of interventions which should be taken into account. In so far as the first and second are arguments about an individual's perception of themselves they can be construed as coherent grievances. How conclusive they are as objections to action is another question and will depend on the weight given to this argument in comparison with other arguments for and against gene therapy. It would be possible, for example, given appropriate technology, to construct an argument for gene therapy as a means to *preserve* an individual's sense of self, for example, for an individual at risk of premature Alzheimer's disease. One point to note here is that this objection is no longer limited to being an objection to germ-line therapy; somatic therapy also would be subject to this objection – and indeed certain nongenetic interventions such as cochlear implants in the case of deafness. In so far as the latter is true, it highlights the possible irrelevance of genetics to issues of personal identity under this interpretation.

What these possible grievances should highlight is the inadequacy of giving our attention to identity issues only in the deep sense of identity as opposed to the individual's selfperception. Alasdair MacIntyre (1981) has drawn attention to the inevitable failure of a concentration on issues of 'strict' identity: 'possessing only the resources of psychological continuity, we have to be able to respond to the imputation of strict identity. I am forever whatever I have been at any time for others – and I may be at any time called upon to answer for it – no matter how changed I may be now'. The concept of a person is an abstraction: 'the characters in a history are not a collection of persons, but the concept of a person is that of a character abstracted from a history' (MacIntyre 1981).

This narrative conception of the self also has implications for gene therapy via the concept of collective identity. This is a further sense in which it might be said to be of concern that we interfere at the genetic level. First there is collective identity as *a species*. Nelkin and Lindee (1995), having suggested that DNA is the secular equivalent of soul stuff, proceed to suggest that our genes are seen as defining us as a species – distinct from others – of those who share our DNA. This is yet another sense in which DNA may be seen as definitive of identity. More pertinent to the present discussion, however, is collective identity of those who share a particular genetic characteristic.

6. Collective Identity

MacIntyre has argued that 'the self has to find its moral identity in and through its membership in communities such as those of the family, the neighborhood, the city and the tribe'

(1981). This may be what is at stake in certain disability rights arguments, where people see their identity intimately associated with a particular condition and group – as in the deaf culture argument, for example. The promise of genetic cures for deafness is seen as a threat to deaf culture (Grundfast and Rosen 1992). A full treatment of this argument requires a consideration not only of personal identity issues but also of issues of justice and of the proper goals of medicine. The essential point for present purposes is that it is crucial to distinguish between arguments that are opposing genetic developments such as gene therapy on the grounds of individual identity, and those which oppose them on the grounds of collective identity. As already mentioned, however, this argument is not confined to genetics, because it has also been applied to cochlear implants.

> **Activity:**
>
> Do you think that there is something special in gene therapy for which it deserves particular consideration?
>
> Is Chadwick correct in thinking that gene therapy is not unique in posing a threat to people's perception of themselves? Consider the point of view of disability rights organisations: do you think that genetic medicine can be seen as a threat and not as a therapy for certain conditions?

Can genetics cause society to become less tolerant?

Now read Ruth Chadwick's conclusions and draw your own conclusions about what you have read.

7. Conclusion

What then can we learn from this? First, that it cannot be established that the essential 'me', my identity in the strict sense, lies in my complete set of genes. It seems implausible to suppose that there could be no change at the genetic level without producing an identity change. Other perspectives locate the essential me elsewhere, such as in psychological characteristics or in character, but the nature of the relationship between genes and these characteristics is controversial, depending as it does on different views about determinism.

Our genes may, however, play an essential part in constructing our sense of self, particularly in so far as we are aware of some essential characteristic. In that case it is the phenotype that becomes important and interventions of a nongenetic kind may be just as threatening as genetic ones. How seriously are we to take the arguments about threats to personal identity as objections to genetic interventions? We have seen that no coherent grievance could be expressed to changes to identity in the strict sense. A coherent objection could be expressed to changes to one's perception of one's identity insofar as it can have serious psychosocial consequences and these have to be taken into account. They do not, however, form a conclusive argument against gene therapy.

Issues of collective identity cannot be resolved via the identity issue alone. They require an examination of issues of justice and the relationship between individual and community. As MacIntyre says, the location of the moral identity of the self in communities 'does not entail that the self has to accept the moral *limitations* of the particularity of those forms of community' (1981).

Chadwick's conclusions seem to suggest that, if we avoid any kind of naïve (philosophically and scientifically) deterministic interpretation of genetic knowledge, we begin to see that it is not genetics *per se* that is the cause for discrimination, exclusion, threats to human identity or other forms of reduction of the human worth. Instead, what is really strategic here is the analysis and discussion of genetics in the wider context of distributive justice and relationships between individuals and communities.

Medical ethics are often criticised for being too practical and even 'too technical' in their approach to ethical issues in clinical medicine and health policy. Reflections on wider and fundamental issues, like the meaning of life, death, suffering, ageing and disease have lost ground to 'technical' solutions to ethical problems of medical technology and practice. A Dutch 'ethicist' claimed some years ago that he was an 'ethical engineer'. The weighing of benefits and burdens and the focus on informed consent are considered important and relevant instruments for ethical analysis. However, in some ways they represent too narrow an approach to ethical problems that doctors and patients and their families are confronted with.

When people are ill, particularly when they are terminally ill, they are very often wrestling with the deeper issues of the meaning of life and the meaning of *their* life, in the light of their disease.

Such fundamental questions may come up in the practice of clinical genetics. A positive test for a gene with a high risk of (a debilitating and terminal) disease may confront the client with questions about his further life. How should he see himself in the light of his genetic condition? Not only people with high genetic risks, but also those who are tested for increased risk or higher susceptibility (for example to cancer or heart disease) are faced with such questions. It is here that philosophical insights, for example on the meaning of personal identity, may help the practitioner to support the client in coping with his genetic condition. This means coping with genetics in his or her private life (change of lifestyle), but also in his or her social life, where discrimination of people with a certain genetic predisposition frequently occurs (like for example with access to insurances). Philosophical perceptions on the role of genetics in our lives ('are we our *defect* genes?') should be part of our approach of the ethical issues raised by genetic testing, screening and research.

Activity:

Consider for a moment the clients in your personal practice: were they confronted with these fundamental questions about the meaning of their lives and the impact of their genetic defects? How did they feel about them? Consider for example the issue of uncertainty of genetic information. How did you approach such a problem: did you discuss such issues with them? How did you discuss them? Does Ruth Chadwick's paper help you to answer the fundamental questions of clients?

Summary

In this chapter we have dealt with the following topics:
- the general features of the most widespread and well-known ethical theories;
- the application of some ethical principles to a specific subject, namely gene therapy, with the aim of showing how

moral reasoning works in practice and how moral arguments may be used in order to address concrete cases;
- the possibility to argue for alternative ways of moral reasoning;
- different outcomes flowing from the application of heterogenous ethical theories.

The fifth and final chapter is aimed at giving basic information about some theoretical concepts in ethics. Some major ethical theories are presented here and the different solutions they offer to genetic issues are discussed. Our goal is that of seeing how ethics works in the field – even when it is proposed as a theory. We wish to provide readers with some concrete examples of philosophical ways of reasoning. Accordingly, Ruth Chadwick's paper on gene therapy is presented as a 'case' of putting moral reasoning into practice. Readers should be empowered with these ethical concepts, that they may be willing to apply to cases, in order to assess the different consequences flowing from them.

Suggestions for further reading

Parens E. (ed.) (1998). *Enhancing Human Traits. Ethical and Social Implications.* Washington D.C.: Georgetown University Press.

Walters L and Palmer J.C.(1997). *The Ethics of Human Gene Therapy.* New York, Oxford: Oxford University Press.

Critical Readers

Professor Inez de Beaufort Department of Medical Ethics and History of Medicine, Erasmus University, Rotterdam, The Netherlands.

Dr Nikola Biller-Andorno Department of Medical Ethics and History of Medicine, University of Göttingen, Göttingen, Germany.

Dr Lucy Frith University of Liverpool, Liverpool, United Kingdom

Dr Ritva Halila General Secretary, National Advisory Board on Health Care Ethics, Helsinki, Finland

Professor Leo ten Kate Department of Clinical Genetics, Free University, Amsterdam, The Netherlands

Claus-Dieter Middel, MA, MPH Institut für Theorie und Geschichte der Medizin, University of Münster, Germany

Dr Michael Parker The Ethox Centre, Institute of Health Sciences, University of Oxford, Oxford, United Kingdom.

Dr Guiseppe Tavormina Studio Medico di Psichiatria, Provaglio d'Iseo, Italy

List of Participants

First Workshop 'Ethics and Genetics', June 9 – 10, 2000 Maastricht, The Netherlands

Professor Luis Archer National Bioethics Committee, Lissabon

Dr Arja Aro National Public Health Institute, Helsinki

Dr Piers Benn Imperial College, London

Professor Donna Dickenson Imperial College, London

Dr Jeantine Lunshof Germany

Professor Ruud ter Meulen Institute for Bioethics, Maastricht

Professor Roberto Mordacci San Raffaele University, Milan

Dr Carmen Rauch Centre d'enseignement et de recherche d'éthique médicale, Marseille

Professor Guido de Wert Institute for Bioethics, Maastricht

Dr Heather Widdows Imperial College, London

Second Workshop 'Ethics and Genetics', November 3 – 4, 2000 Milan, Italy

Professor Luis Archer National Bioethics Committee, Lissabon

Dr Arja Aro National Public Health Institute, Helsinki

Dr. Eleonora Boggio San Raffaele University, Milan

Professor Ruth Chadwick Lancaster University, United Kingdom

Professor Donna Dickenson Imperial College, London

Dr Kris Dierickx Centre for Biomedical Ethics, Louvain

Dr Jeantine Lunshof Germany

Professor Ruud ter Meulen Institute for Bioethics, Maastricht

Dr Roberto Mordacci San Raffaele University, Milan

Dr Carmen Rauch Centre d'enseignement et de recherche d'éthique médicale, Marseille

Professor Guido de Wert Institute for Bioethics, Maastricht

Dr Heather Widdows Imperial College, London

Genetic User Group, 13 September, 2001

Professor Donna Dickenson Imperial College, London

Dr Christine de Die Clinical Genetics, University of Maastricht

Drs. Rob van Hooren University of Maastricht

Drs. Antina de Jong Institute for Bioethics, Maastricht

Drs. Willem Koch University of Maastricht

Professor Ruud ter Meulen Institute for Bioethics, Maastricht

Drs. Theo Niessen University of Maastricht

Dr Connie Schrander Clinical Genetics, University of Maastricht

Drs. Christien Sepers Institute for Bioethics, Maastricht

Esther van Swieten University of Maastricht

Professor Mariachiara Tallaccini San Raffaele University, Milan

Saskia Tromp University of Maastricht

Professor Guido de Wert Institute for Bioethics, Maastricht

Dr Heather Widdows Imperial College, London

References

Adams, J. (1990). Confidentiality and Huntington's chorea. *J Med Ethics,* **16**: 196–199.

American Society of Clinical Oncology (1996). Statement of the American Society of Clinical Oncology: Genetic testing for cancer susceptibility. *Journal of Clinical Oncology* **14**: 1730–6.

American Society of Human Genetics (1975). Genetic Counseling. *American Journal of Human Genetics*: 140–142.

Andrews, L.B., Fullarton J.E., Holtzman N.A. and Motulsky A.G. (eds) (1994). *Assessing genetic risks. Implications for health and social policy.* Washington D.C.: National Academy Press.

Annas, G.J. (2000). Rules for research on human genetic variation – lessons from Iceland. *New England Journal of Medicine*, **342**:1830–1833.

Arras, J.D. (1990). AIDS and reproductive decisions: having children in fear and trembling. *The Milbank Quarterly*, **68**: 353–382.

Baird, P.A. (1990). Opportunity and danger: medical, ethical and social implications of early DNA screening for identification of genetic risk of common adult onset disorders. In *Genetic screening.* B.M. Knoppers and C.M. Laberge, (eds), Amsterdam: Excerpta Medica, pp. 279–87.

British Medical Association (1998). *Human Genetics. Choice and Responsibility.* Oxford: Oxford University Press.

Brock, D. (1995). The non-identity problem and genetic harm. *Bioethics,* **9**: 269–276.

Buchanan, A., Brock, D.W., Daniels, N. and Wikler, D. (2000) *From chance to choice. Genetics & Justice.* Cambridge: Cambridge University Press.

Chadwick, R.F. (1987) The perfect baby: Introduction. In *Id., ed., Ethics, Reproduction and Genetic control,* London, New York: Routledge, pp. 93–136.

Chadwick, R. (1998). Gene therapy. In *A Companion to Bioethics,* H. Kuhse, and P. Singer, (eds), Oxford: Blackwell, pp. 189–197.

Chadwick, R. (1991) The Iceland database: so modern times need modern sagas? *British Medical Journal,* **319**: 441–444.

Chadwick, R., Levitt, M.A. and Shickle, D. (eds) (1997) *The Right to Know and the Right not to Know.* Aldershot: Avebury.

Chadwick, R., (1998). Genetic Screening and Ethics: European Perspectives. *Journal of Medicine and Philosophy,* **23**: 255–273.

Clothier, Cecil (1992), *Report of the Committee on the Ethics of Gene Therapy*. London: HMSO.

Core Committee Ethics of Medical Research (1993). Annual Report 1991 and 1992. The Hague: Health Council of the Netherlands, (in Dutch).

Council of Europe (1996). Convention for the protection of human rights and dignity of the human being with regard to the application of biology and medicine: Convention on Human Rights and Biomedicine. Directorate of Legal Affairs, Strasbourg, November.

DeGrazia, D. (1991). The ethical justification for minimal paternalism in the use of the predictive test for Huntington's disease. *The Journal of Clinical Ethics*, **2**: 219–28.

Directive 98/44/EC of the European Parliament and of the Council of 6 July 1998 on the legal protection of biotechnological inventions, OJL 213, 30/7/1998, pp.13–21.

Elliott, Robert (1993), Identity and the Ethics of Gene Therapy. *Bioethics*, 7: 27–40.

Embryo Protection Act 1990. December 1990 (BGBI.I S.2746) (in German).

European Commission, Opinions of the Group of Advisers on the Ethical Implications of Biotechnology to the European Commission 1991–1997, European Commission, Secretariat-General, 1997.

European Society of Human Genetics (2000). Public and Professional Policy Committee. EUROGAPPP Project 1999–2000, Population Genetic Screening Programmes: Principles, Techniques, Practices, and Policies.

Farrar, S. (1999). UK considers national gene database. *Times Higher Education Supplement*, **11**: February.

Fears, R. and Poste, G. (1999). Building population genetics resources using the U.K. NHS. *Science*, **284**: 267–8.

Geller, G., Botkin, J.R., and Green, M.J. et al. (1997). Genetic testing for susceptibility to adult-onset cancer. The process and content of informed consent. (Consensus Statement) *JAMA*, **277**: 1467–1474.

Gilbert, W. (1992). A Vision of the Grail. In *The Code of Codes: Scientific and Social Issues in the Human Genome Project*, Daniel J. Kevles and Leroy Hood (eds),. Cambridge, Mass: Harvard University Press.

Grundfast, Kenneth M. and Rosen, Jeffrey (1992). Ethical and Cultural Considerations in Research on Hereditary Deafness. *Molecular Biology and Genetics*, **25**(5): 973.

Harris, J. (1992). *Wonderwoman and Superman: The Ethics of Human Biotechnology*. Oxford: Oxford University Press.

Helpdesk Gezondheid en Verzekeringen, Breed Platform Verzekerden en Werk (2001). *Helderheid gewenst. Rapportage 2000*, Amsterdam.

Holtzman, N.A. and Watson, M.S. (eds) (1998). *Promoting Safe and Effective Genetic Testing in the United States.* Baltimore-London: The Johns Hopkins University Press.

Human Genome Organisation. Ethics Committee(1996). Statement on the Principled Conduct of Genetic Research. *Genome Digest* **3**: 2–3.

Human Genome Organisation. Ethics Committee. Statement on Benefit Sharing. 2000.

International Huntington Association and World Federation of Neurology (1994). Guidelines for the molecular genetics predictive test in Huntington's disease. *Neurology,* **44**: 1533–1536.

Jasanoff S. (1995). *Science at the Bar. Law, Science, and Technology in America.* Cambridge Ma: Harvard University Press.

Law on Medical Examinations, 1997 (in Dutch).

Ledger GA, Khosla S, Lindor NM, et al. (1995). Genetic testing in the diagnosis and management of multiple endocrine neoplasia type II. *Annuals of Internal Medicine,* **122**:118–224.

MacIntyre, A. (1981). *After Virtue: A Study in Moral Theory.* London: Duckworth.

McGleenan, T. (2000). Legal and Policy Issues in Genetics and Insurance. *Community Genetics,* **3**: 45–49.

McLaren A. (1997). A note on 'totipotency'. *Biomedical Ethics. Newsletter of the European Network for Biomedical Ethics,* **2** (1): 7.

Medical Research Council (1999). *Human Tissue and Biological Samples for Use in Research: Report of the Medical Research Council Working Group to Develop Operational and Ethical Guidelines.*

Meijers-Heijboer H., Van Geel B, Van Putten W, et al. (2001). Breast cancer after prophylactic bilateral mastectomy in women with a BRCA1 or BRCA2 mutation. *New England Journal of Medicine* **345**:159–164.

Ter Meulen R., Van der Made J. (2000). The extent and limits of solidarity in Dutch health care. *International Journal of Social Welfare,* **9**: 250–260.

Michie S. (1996) Predictive testing in children: paternalism or empiricism? In *The troubled helix. Social and psychological implications of the new human genetics,* Th. Marteau and M. Richards, (eds), Cambridge: Cambridge University Press, pp.177–183.

Miller, Hugh III (1998). DNA Blueprints, Personhood, and Genetic Privacy. *Health Matrix,* **8** (2): 179–221.

Morrison Institute for Population and Resource Studies(1997). Model Ethical Protocol for Collecting DNA Samples (North American Regional Committee – Human Genome Diversity Project).

Motulsky A. (1997). Screening for Genetic Diseases. *New England Journal of Medicine,* **336** (18): 1314–1316.

Nairne P.(1995). Genetic screening 1. In *Parliaments and Screening – Ethical and social problems arising from testing and screening for HIV and genetic disease,* K. Wayland (ed.), Paris: John Libbey Eurotext, pp. 59–64.

National Bioethics Advisory Commission (1999). *Research Involving Human Biological Materials: Ethical Issues and Policy Guidance.* Rockville, Maryland.

National Bioethics Advisory Commission (2000). *Ethical and Policy Issues in International Resarch.* Bethesda, Maryland.

Nelkin D. and Lindee, M.S. (1995). *The DNA Mystique: the gene as cultural icon.* New York: W.H.Freeman.

NIH Consensus Development Conference on Genetic Testing for Cystic Fibrosis, 1997.

North Cumbria Community Genetics Project (2000). *Report 1996–2000.*

Nuffield Council on Bioethics (1993). *Genetic Screening. Ethical Issues.* London.

Post S.(1991). Selective abortion and gene therapy: reflections on human limits. *Human Gene Therapy,* **2**: 229–233.

Pottage, A. (1998). The Inscription of Life in Law: Genes, Patents, and Bio-Politics. *Modern Law Review,* **61**(5): 740 –765.

President's Commission (1983). *Screening and counselling for genetic conditions. The ethical, social, and legal implications of genetic screening, counselling, and education programs.* Washington D.C.: U.S. GPO.

Robertson JA. (1992). Ethical and legal issues in preimplantaton genetic screening. *Fertility and Sterility,* **57**: 1–11.

Robertson JA. (1994). *Children of Choice. Freedom and the New Reproductive Technologies.* Princeton, NJ: Princeton University Press.

Royal Dutch Society of Physicians: Ethics Committee (1997). *Doctors and Genes. The use of genetic knowledge in medical practice.* Utrecht: (in Dutch).

Schneider, H. and Coutelle, C. (1999). In utero Gene Therapy: The Case for. *Nature Medicine,* **5**(3): 256–257.

Schulman J, Black S, Handyside A, Nance W. (1996). Preimplantation genetic testing for Huntington disease and certain other dominantly inherited disorders. *Clinical Genetics* **49**: 57–58.

Seibel M.M., Seibel S.G., Zilberstein M. (1994). Gender distribution – not sex selection. *Human Reproduction,* **9**: 569–570.

Simpson J.L. and Liebaers I. (1996). Assessing congenital anomalies after preimplantation genetic diagnosis. *Journal of Assisted Reproduction and Genetics,* **13**: 170–176.

Singer P. and Wells D. (1984). *The Reproduction Revolution. New Ways of Making Babies.* Oxford: Oxford University Press.

Smith R. and Wynne B. (eds) (1989). *Expert Evidence: Interpreting Science in the Law.* London: Routledge.

Society for Human Genetics (Gesellschaft für Humangenetik) (1996). Position Paper. *Medizinische Genetik*, **8**: 125–131 (in German).

De Sola C. (1995). Privacy and Genetic Data. Cases of Conflict (II). *Law and the Human Genome Review*, **2**: 147–156.

Solovitch S. (2001). The Citizen Scientists, *Wired*, http://www.wired.com/wired/archive/9.09/disease.html (accessed September 2001)

Specter M. (1991). Decoding Iceland. *New Yorker*, (1) 41–51.

Stacey, J. (1997). *Teratologies: A Cultural Study of Cancer*. London: Routledge.

Stranc L. and Evans J. (1998), Issues Relating to the Implementation of Genetic Screening Programs, in *SocioEthical Issues in Human Genetics*, B.M. Knoppers, (ed.), Cowansville Québec: Les Editions Yvon Blais Inc, pp. 49–105.

Strathern, M. (1992). *Reproducing the Future: Essays on Anthropology, Kinship, and the New Reproductive Technologies*. Manchester: Manchester University Press.

Strong C. (1997). *Ethics in reproductive and perinatal medicine. A new framework*. New Haven, London: Yale University Press.

Tilanus-Linthorst M.M. (2000). First experiences in screening women at high risk for breast cancer with MR imaging. *Breast Cancer Research and Treatment*, **63**: 53–66.

UNESCO Universal Declaration on the Human Genome and the Human Rights, 1997.

Weijer C. (1999). Protecting communities in research: philosophical and pragmatic challenges. *Cambridge Quarterly of Healthcare Ethics*, **8**: 501–513.

De Wert G. (1998). Ethics of predictive DNA-testing for hereditary breast and ovarian cancer. *Patient Education and Counseling*, **35**: 43–52.

De Wert G. (1999a). Ethics of assisted reproduction: the case of preimplantation genetic diagnosis. In *Molecular Biology in Reproductive Medicine*, B.C.J.M. Fauser, J.F. Straus and A. van Steirteghem, (eds), New York, London: Parthenon, pp. 433–448.

De Wert G. (1999b). *With a view to the future. Reproductive technologies, genetics and ethics*. Amsterdam: Thela Thesis (in Dutch).

Williams B. (1990). Who might I have been? In *Human Genetic Information: science, law and ethics*, D.J. Chatwick and G.R. Bock (eds), Chichester: Wiley, pp.176–173.

Wet Medische Keuringen (Law Medical Examinations), 1997, www.minvws.nl.

Yarborough M., Scott J.A. and Dixon L.K. (1989). The role of beneficence in clinical genetics: non-directive counselling reconsidered. *Theoretical Medicine*, **10**: 139–149.

Index

DATE DUE
